Cambridge Elements

Elements in Environmental Humanities
edited by
Louise Westling
University of Oregon
Serenella Iovino
University of North Carolina at Chapel Hill
Timo Maran
University of Tartu

THE ENVIRONMENTAL HUMANITIES AND THE ANCIENT WORLD

Questions and Perspectives

Christopher Schliephake
University of Augsburg

T0364231

CAMBRIDGE
UNIVERSITY PRESS

CAMBRIDGE
UNIVERSITY PRESS

University Printing House, Cambridge CB2 8BS, United Kingdom

One Liberty Plaza, 20th Floor, New York, NY 10006, USA

477 Williamstown Road, Port Melbourne, VIC 3207, Australia

314–321, 3rd Floor, Plot 3, Splendor Forum, Jasola District Centre,
New Delhi – 110025, India

79 Anson Road, #06–04/06, Singapore 079906

Cambridge University Press is part of the University of Cambridge.

It furthers the University's mission by disseminating knowledge in the pursuit of
education, learning, and research at the highest international levels of excellence.

www.cambridge.org
Information on this title: www.cambridge.org/9781108749046
DOI: 10.1017/9781108782005

First published 2020

A catalogue record for this publication is available from the British Library.

ISBN 978-1-108-74904-6 Paperback
ISSN 2632-3125 (online)
ISSN 2632-3117 (print)

The Environmental Humanities and the Ancient World

Questions and Perspectives

Elements in Environmental Humanities

DOI: 10.1017/9781108782005
First published online: June 2020

Christopher Schliephake
University of Augsburg

Author for correspondence: Christopher Schliephake, christopher.schliepha
ke@philhist.uni-augsburg.de

Abstract: What can a study of antiquity contribute to the interdisciplinary paradigm of the environmental humanities? And how does this recent paradigm influence the way we perceive human–"nature" interactions in premodernity? By asking these and a number of related questions, this Element aims to show why the ancient tradition still matters in the Anthropocene. Offering new perspectives to think about what directions the ecological turn could take in classical studies, it revisits old material, including ancient Greek religion and mythology, with central concepts of contemporary environmental theory. It also critically engages with forms of classical reception in current debates, arguing that ancient ecological knowledge is a powerful resource for creating alternative worldviews.

Keywords: Anthropocene, antiquity, ecology, myth, environment

JEL classifications:

ISBNs: 9781108749046 (PB), 9781108782005 (OC)
ISSNs: 2632-3125 (online), 2632–3117 (print)

Contents

1 Introduction

What is the place of the ancient *anthropos* in the Anthropocene?

Finding ways to reflect on this question will be one of the main aims of this Element. To make it clear from the outset: there are no straight answers. For one thing, this has to do with the slippery notion of the Anthropocene. There are no agreed-upon definitions of the term from a chronological, geological, or political vantage point. At the same time, the ancient *anthropos* is nothing more than a construct. It is a convenient shorthand for subsuming widely differing cultures, peoples, and epochs under a common banner. So, when I speak of the ancient world, or the ancient *anthropos*, this has to be taken with a pinch of salt.

Antiquity was neither a homogeneous nor a culturally universal epoch. Rather, it encompassed millennia, reaching all the way from the Bronze Age to the spread of Islam in the seventh century CE. This volume will mainly focus on Greco-Roman antiquity, incorporating sources from what is commonly referred to as the archaic (ca. eighth to sixth centuries BCE) and the classical Greek world (ca. fifth to fourth centuries BCE), the Hellenistic period (ca. 323–30 BCE), and the Roman Imperial period (ca. 30 BCE to 284 CE). There were, of course, other much older cultures, like the Egyptians or the cultures of the Near East, that had an immense influence on the ancient Mediterranean. And, despite the great significance that the Greco-Roman world had for modern conceptualizations of the "West," or, indeed, conceptions of the "human," it should be made clear from the outset that, when I speak of the classical world, my pathway differs from forms of reception that are interested in the "universalism" or normativity of tradition.

Rather, the following pages will try to perceive the Greco-Roman world against the background of its own particular place and context in human history. My Element will be concerned with establishing a dialogue with this world. Keeping the main question posed at the outset in mind, it will center around a number of related questions that will entail different theoretical problems and that will demand specific methodological approaches. The main goal will be to illustrate the role that antiquity can play in the interdisciplinary paradigm of the environmental humanities and to come up with perspectives for further dialogues. The study is aimed at practitioners in the environmental humanities who have so far predominantly focused on modernity but who are interested in gaining a deeper historical perspective on socio-ecological interrelationships in the Mediterranean as well as classical scholars who may have worked on ancient environments but who have not yet incorporated theoretical or methodological models of contemporary environmental theory into their research. In order to lay the ground for this encounter, the Introduction will give an overview of the state of the discussion at this point in time, and it will do so by starting with the most problematic of all terms: the Anthropocene.

The Anthropocene

The Anthropocene has raised much attention. In recent memory, no other word has led to a comparable degree of interdisciplinary debate. Be it the sciences, the social sciences, the humanities, or the media – it seems that everybody has had their say in discussing the term's many connotations and implications, most of which are still unclear. The starting point of the debate can be found in earth system science and the realization that the human species is about to transcend certain limits set by the global ecosystem, including the availability of natural resources. There are a number of precursors to the word "Anthropocene" (Zalasiewicz et al. 2010), but it was only when the atmospheric chemist Paul J. Crutzen, together with the biologist Eugene F. Stoermer, popularized the notion at the turn of the twenty-first century that it met with a reverberating echo across the sciences and the media.

According to Crutzen and Stoermer (2000), the term describes a new geological epoch in the history of planet Earth. While it denotes recent developments, its linguistic roots reach deeper: the word is a combination of the ancient Greek *anthropo-* (from *anthropos*, "human") and *-cene* (from *kainos*, "new" or "recent"). Anthropocene, then, is born from the realization that "the human imprint on the global environment has now become so large and active that it rivals some of the great forces of Nature in its impact on the functioning of the Earth system" (Steffen et al. 2011: 842). With its focus on anthropogenic effects on the nonhuman environment and its planetary scale, the notion has stirred a lot of interest but also a wide range of interpretations, along with a fair share of controversy.

One problem consists in the word's inherent anthropocentrism. There is a tendency toward discursively appropriating the Earth and relegating all other living beings and nonhuman matter to the margins of an otherwise human-controlled environment. The Anthropocene discourse is divided between a "bad" version and a "good" version. While the first one brings with it a baggage of apocalyptic imagery and dystopian doomsday scenarios, eventually leading to the imagined collapse of the life-supporting planetary system, the second is freighted with the fantasy of omnipotence, namely of being able to master and to finally manage adverse environmental effects, for instance with the help of climate engineering (Dalby 2016). Both versions make "humankind" the yardstick against which to measure environmental health and well-being.

Another problem is that the Anthropocene has the suggestive power of a collective singular; that is, it tends to cover up cultural, historical, political, and socioeconomic disparity and heterogeneity. Talk of the "human era" (Schwägerl 2014) is misleading in so far as it is not all humans who have turned into a global environmental factor but a certain type of human, defined by a certain degree of material prosperity and political agency. As the Indian novelist Amitav Ghosh argues, both capitalism and the history of empire, namely imperialism, are among the root causes of many environmental perils so characteristic of our times, including climate change (2016: 87).

While this crisis is usually framed in techno-scientific terms, whereby certain types of energy use or resource management are seen as the main ecological problems, history and politics are often pushed to the background. Yet, above all, human decision-making and human choices have opted for the use of certain technologies and/or resources (not vice versa). And these decision-makers and processes can be identified in historical analysis. As Rob Nixon (2014) puts it, "We may all be in the Anthropocene but we're not all in it in the same way." Nixon thereby points to the socioeconomic and cultural-historical asymmetry inherent in our current ecological crisis – and to the need to come up with different perspectives and narratives.

It is at this point that the new paradigm of the "environmental humanities" comes into play as an important scholarly intervention. "The environmental humanities," writes Ursula Heise in a recent introduction into the field, "envision ecological crises fundamentally as questions of socioeconomic inequality, cultural difference, and divergent histories, values and ethical frameworks." As she posits, "Scientific understanding and technological problem-solving, essential though they are, themselves are shaped by such frameworks and stand to gain by situating themselves in the historical and sociocultural landscape" (Heise 2017: 2).

It is therefore not so much a question of whether the humanities should grapple with the notion of the Anthropocene at all as, rather, of what stance they should take in the face of its many challenges. Without question, the word offers itself as a starting point for interdisciplinary debate and reflection that take social as well as material aspects and their interactive enmeshment into account as grounding principles of human–nature interaction. The term helps render the codependency of environment, politics, and technology, uniting many factors usually analyzed in isolation. Due to the various chronological, geological, and human "scales" involved, the Anthropocene is, in the words of Timothy Clark (2015), a "threshold concept," prompting new ways of thinking short-term developments and deep-historical processes together.

This last aspect touches upon the third big challenge connected to the "new human era": namely, the question of when it, in fact, begins. Early approaches, including those of Stoermer and Crutzen, preferred the beginning of the Industrial Revolution around 1800.[1] However, technically speaking, a new era needs to have lasting imprints on the Earth's strata in order to qualify as a geological epoch. That is why a new generation of scholars prefer the first atomic tests and the use of nuclear weapons in 1945 as a critical watershed. The spread of radionuclides goes hand-in-hand with the so-called "Great Acceleration" in the aftermath of World War II, which saw a rapid increase in resource extraction and the global use of pesticides (Zalasiewicz et al. 2016).

Thus, from a geological vantage point, it is clear that antiquity clearly falls outside the chronological markers of the Anthropocene. Although we lack quantifiable statistics, we can safely say that the ancient population numbers were a long way from modern-day standards. Moreover, ancient people did not rely on the same amount of resources, and they did not know the deleterious effects of radioactivity, chemicals, or plastic waste. Antiquity saw neither an "industrialization" in the narrow sense of the term nor a technologization. So, why bother at all with whether the ancients have, or should have, a place in the Anthropocene?

I think there are good reasons why we, indeed, should think about how the Anthropocene, as a historical era, relates to other time periods. And these have to do with different types of "scale": because if dealing with the Anthropocene means coming to terms with the convergence of different scales, be they of a chronological (natural vs. human history), a normative (the human vs. the nonhuman), or a geographical (planet vs. region) type, then antiquity belongs to the other end of the spectrum of the many dystopian scenarios connected to the "human era." For the Indian historian Dipesh Chakrabarty (2009: 197–198), the future has turned into a domain detached from historical consciousness, a realm that no longer stands in any kind of continuity with the past.

However, one could also invert this perspective and suggest that antiquity itself belongs in a realm of human experience that constantly challenges and tests the limits of the historical imagination and of historical understanding.

---

[1] There are also voices claiming that the Anthropocene begins with the encounter between the "old" and "new" worlds and the discovery of the American continent in 1492, because it set in motion a process of species exchange unthinkable without anthropogenic influence. The idea that the Anthropocene may be even older, and that it began in practice with the first extensive proto-urban settlements in Mesopotamia around 5,000 BCE or even with the rise of agriculture around 10,000 BCE, is also discussed (Ruddiman 2003). The question of whether Greco-Roman sources express ideologies of a human dominance over nature or bemoan negative anthropogenic effects on the environment – two aspects that would allow us to see them as prefiguring debates surrounding the term "Anthropocene" – will be dealt with in the course of this Element.

Chronologically speaking, antiquity makes up the deep perspective of historical consciousness. The period already saw phenomena like catastrophe, collapse, and regeneration – including in environmental terms. One could even say that the popular narrative of the Anthropocene, presented in countless articles and books, makes use of the generic structure of rise-and-fall narratives inspired by ancient models and elaborated in (early) modern historiography.

If we, in consequence, consider that the ancients had a vital interest in the mutability of passages of time and a sensibility to the succession of eras,[2] then it becomes clear that our modern debates hark back to ancient examples. One could say that, culturally speaking, an Anthropocene existed long before its geological and material effects became apparent. One of the oldest (fragmentary) texts of world literature, the Gilgamesh epic, already spoke of the divide between an urbanized "culture" and wild "nature," reflecting on the benefits and the eventual pitfalls of making use of the Earth's resources (Dalley 2017). That same frontier spirit can be found in Odysseus' encounter with the fabled Cyclopes, who apparently live in harmony with the environment but are still unable to make use of its abundant riches (Homer *Odyssey* 9, 108–118). Roman writers celebrated the triumph of human culture over "nature" (Thommen 2012: 76–78). The list goes on.

These examples aside, I would argue that it is one of the most important challenges of the environmental humanities to confront the geological or natural-historical perspective of the prevalent Anthropocene discourse with the implications and challenges of a cultural deep history. This entails the need to reactivate the contents of our cultural memory in current debates (Westling & Parham 2017). In other words, we should be wary of turning the environmental humanities into Anthropocene studies, with a narrow focus on modernity and the (post)industrial age. Rather, we also have to track the Anthropocene and its ideology in the deep structures of human history and imagination. What were the channels, media, and images that saw its rise in premodernity? Again, there are no straight answers, but this is a worthwhile task, because what we will encounter are not only anthropocentric perspectives but also worldviews and metaphors that will help undermine them, that will confront us with wholly different outlooks on what it means to live in a material world and, indeed, what it means to be human in it.

Methodologically speaking, this also entails the necessity of tracing the material, social, and cultural forms of culture–nature interaction in the deep strata of the past. "Strata" is, of course, a geological term. It refers to the

---

[2] In ancient Greece, there were two popular variants of cultural theories, one that perceived culture as steadily declining (i.e. a theory of descendancy) and one that saw it as constantly evolving (i.e. a theory of ascendancy). Cf. Vögler 2000: 242–243.

different measurable effects of the Anthropocene in the so-called lithosphere, the atmosphere, the biosphere, and the sociosphere (Zalasiewicz 2016). There is, however, also a cultural sphere that acts like a seismograph and interprets tangible changes in any one of those spheres in a context-dependent way. These cultural feedback effects are integral parts of an environmental history that investigates human–nature interactions in premodernity.

However, it is also important to bear in mind the possibilities and limits of comparative history. The attempt to draw comparisons between our modern age and its ecological crises and the ancient sources can easily lead to anachronisms; and any attempt to draw conclusions from a reading of ancient texts for our current predicaments will, most likely, be doomed to fail. These cautionary notes notwithstanding, what is possible is to attempt to determine the place of both modern and ancient humankind in a natural history whose trajectories have been anything but clear or predetermined. In doing so, we are confronted with the limits of historical understanding, on the one hand, and of human agency, on the other, thereby also problematizing the ethical implications of the Anthropocene.

The Environmental Humanities and the Ancient World

It is probably no coincidence that around the same time as Stoermer and Crutzen formulated their concept of the Anthropocene in the year 2000, there was increasing talk of a new academic field, devoted to dealing with environmental questions in an interdisciplinary way that saw ecological and cultural issues as inextricably intertwined. Drawing on environmental studies programs and approaches in environmental history, philosophy, literary and cultural studies, as well as anthropology and the social sciences, that had separately developed during the second half of the twentieth century, the early years of the twenty-first century were increasingly characterized by a tendency to merge these distinct approaches. What united them in the first place was the growing awareness that the environmental challenges facing life on Earth entailed many ethical, social, and technological questions that could not be solved by the narrow outlook of a single discipline. The humanities and social sciences thereby repositioned their respective roles in academia and their stance regarding the nonhuman world. What had once served as a mere backdrop to the traditional focus on human decision- and meaning-making now came to the fore as central to human ways of being in the world; in fact, closely connected to questions of politics and justice.

Quickly, study programs and institutes emerged all around the globe that adapted the newly coined term "environmental humanities." Although this term is now commonly accepted and widely used, it is still hard to come up with a univocal definition. Due to the many academic disciplines involved, their respective histories and methodologies, as well as distinct national or culture-specific ways of dealing with and perceiving the nonhuman world, the environmental humanities are, indeed, characterized by a high degree of diversity and heterogeneity. As the editors of the journal *Environmental Humanities* put it in their first issue, "the environmental humanities can be understood to be a wide ranging response to the environmental challenges of our time" that ". . . engages with fundamental questions of meaning, value, responsibility and purpose in a time of rapid, and escalating, change" (Rose et al. 2012: 1). The authors of one of the first monograph introductions to the field also point to its multifaceted and wide-ranging approach, listing its historical perspective, its focus on ethics, social justice, and action, and its transdisciplinary and transnational take on environmental issues as defining features (Emmett & Nye 2017: 2–7).

In general, the humanities are thereby perceived "as an imaginative force for thinking about the ongoing evolutionary transformations of the world and its inhabitants" (Adamson 2016: 139). Nonetheless, the traditional way of starting an inquiry into (human) nature from one discipline, e.g. from philosophy or history, and largely remaining within its specialist domains is increasingly seen as insufficient (Emmett & Nye 2017: 21). This has to do with many of the cultural factors that are perceived as root causes of the environmental crisis in the first place: to overcome "the divisive epistemologies that create an illusory sense of an ontological dissociation between the human and the nonhuman realms" (Oppermann & Iovino 2017: 4) is, in this context, one of the main aims connected to the project of the environmental humanities. What were, at one time, dearly held notions of humanities research – for instance, the strict separation between "nature" and "culture," human and animal – have, against this background, become problematized in order to undermine forms of anthropocentrism that have cared little for other life-forms or the biosphere and to create ample space for an interdisciplinary dialogue with the sciences.

The hope is that, through this blurring of traditional boundaries, core elements and key issues of humanities thinking, like ethical reasoning, questions of justice, and meaning, will enter "environmental domains" (Rose et al. 2012: 2) that have, thus far, been characterized by techno-scientific approaches. Thereby, it will, ideally, become possible "to articulate a 'thicker' notion of humanity, one that rejects reductionist accounts of self-contained, rational, decision making subjects" (2). In sum, "the environmental humanities positions us as participants in lively ecologies of meaning and value, entangled with rich patterns of cultural and historical diversity that shape who we are and the ways in which we are able to 'become with' others" (2).

Notwithstanding the weight that these quotations give to the historical perspective engrained in the humanities, it is interesting to note that the premodern
world has predominantly been relegated to the sidelines of the discussion. Of
the many articles and chapters gathered in the introductory anthologies that
have appeared from major presses over the last couple of years, almost none
include the ancient or medieval worlds.[3] Why is this? I would argue that this
has, on the one hand, to do with the urgency of the global ecological crisis.
Although there are no quick solutions to our environmental problems, they
certainly demand of everyone to be constructively involved in shaping better
living conditions and possibilities for present and future generations. In the
humanities, there is probably no one who would seriously question the claim
that the premodern textual and artistic canon upon which our own disciplines
rest should be part of this very future. Integrating this vast body of knowledge
into the discussion and bringing the alternative ecological worldviews stored in
ancient texts to bear on present concerns is a different story altogether. This is an
aspect where more could be done. On the other hand, there are comparatively
few classical philologists, ancient historians, or archaeologists involved in the
debate – despite excellent work on environmental or ecological questions in all
these fields.

It is one of the aims of this Element to help bridge the divide that currently
exists between the environmental humanities, as they now present themselves,
and approaches in classical studies (including ancient history and
archaeology).[4] Why is it important to grant them a more prominent place in
our discussions? Needless to say, the ancient civilizations were themselves
confronted with environmental problems on various scales – some of which
were self-made and some of which were naturally caused (Hughes 2014). There
was also a long tradition of thinking about the interaction and relationships
between humans and their respective environments, reaching back to the earliest written sources alluded to earlier. But these points are probably too obvious
to mention; they are well discussed and undisputed. There is yet another, more
important reason why we should constantly be concerned with the deep past of
human culture. As Greg Garrard puts it, at the core of the environmental

---

[3] My own edited volume on antiquity and ecocriticism (Schliephake 2017a) was an attempt to
   bridge classical scholarship and more recent approaches in the environmental humanities.
   Siewers (2014) and Cohen (2012) have, in their respective works, made important contributions
   that include the medieval world. For a diachronic perspective on the environmental imagination
   and literature, see Westling & Parham (2017).

[4] Although I include some archaeological studies and material in this work, it should be noted that
   another Element would be needed to accompany the present one from a decidedly specialist
   archaeological perspective.

humanities is the dual project of what he terms "the historicization of ecology" and "the ecologization of history" (Garrard 2014: 3–5).

Indeed, in ecological terms, the roots of our environmental crisis reach back very far in time. According to the ecologist Wolfgang Haber, the urban systems of premodern Mesopotamia present the first instance in history when humankind centralized vast natural resources, transforming them into culture (Haber 2016: 29). This transformation, namely centralization, was not unproblematic, however, especially when perceived in the *longue durée*; it brought with it numerous "ecological traps" (Haber 2007), which were integral to the rise of the great ancient cultures but had unintended long-term effects that we still experience today. The discovery, and eventual mastery, of fire was such a milestone in human development because it supplemented the sun's energy and substantially enlarged the diet.

As the ancient Greeks well knew, however, this came at a price. When we think of the myth of Prometheus, who was largely associated with the fire element, it becomes clear that, in ecological terms, technology and knowledge are always accompanied by rebound effects. Developing knowledge and understanding of one's environment and of oneself was a cornerstone of early Greek philosophy, and Prometheus became an exemplary case for reflecting on what this could entail. Fire enables technology and scientific development, as the mythological hero explains in one of the earliest extant tragedies (Aeschylus *Prometheus Bound* 450–471, 476–506), but the gifts and *technai* that Prometheus brings can eventually also lead to suffering – after all, he himself pays the price for transcending divine limits.

While Prometheus' fate can be read as reflective of what happens to someone whose own thirst for knowledge can lead to hardheadedness and subsequent downfall, it also mirrors a deep-seated interest in how the understanding and mastering of natural forces has lasting effects upon the nonhuman world. As Haber notes, "For living matter . . . fire is principally destructive and even lethal, and humans also learned to make use of it in order to get rid of all what disturbed or threatened them" (2007: 359). Moreover,

> Humans soon discovered that the highest energy amount was released by burning wood. Stands of woody plants, i.e. forests, thus were assigned the purpose of providing fuel, and in this way humans created their first and unconditional dependence on a specific natural resource supplying high-grade energy, expecting it to be available forever. This was our first and irreversible step into an ecological trap, because the demand for such an energy source would rise infinitely. (360)

This is an example of how human resource use, ancient mythological insights, and modern science can enter into a dialogue in present accounts, laying bare a deep history of nature–culture interaction that still has serious ramifications for the current ecological crisis.

This only becomes possible, however, when the perspective is broadened beyond the scope of the Anthropocene or the Early Modern era. It is here that we find the roots of our present predicaments, and here we also find some of the "instruments," to paraphrase Joni Adamson, that help us "see" through their manifold entanglements and their connections with our own age (2016: 136). In this case, these "seeing instruments" come to us via the way of an ancient mythological figure – Prometheus, for instance, is an apt mythology for our own times in the Anthropocene. As Irby-Massie notes, "Prometheus' gifts to the human kind include knowledge of the means whereby humanity can protect itself against all blights, but Prometheus himself is the proverbial physician who lacks the remedies with which to heal himself" (2008: 143). This image is highly evocative of the role of techno-scientific knowledge and the uncontrollable nonhuman "species of trouble" (Erikson 1991), e.g. radioactivity, by which it is accompanied in our times.

In his influential essay "The Climate of History: Four Theses" (2009), Chakrabarty has reflected on these unintended consequences of human–nature interaction and their effects on our general understanding of history. He argues that the scope and impact of, for instance, climate change pose serious problems for historians (and humanists in general) because they demand a reconceptualization of many fundamental categories, like race, class, or gender, and because they embed these sociocultural traits within a context of geohistory, where different scales apply in both a chronological and a geological sense. What comes to the fore in this reconceptualization is, firstly, humans' agency as a species and, secondly, the sense that nature has a history too; that it, in fact, "is dynamic, fluctuating, hybrid, and permeable both *in itself* and in relation to corresponding human histories" (Westling & Parham 2017: 5; emphasis in original). In consequence, Heise sees a conceptual tension at work in the environmental humanities in general, and in historical approaches to the field in particular: a "tension between humans' agency as a species and the inequalities that shape and constrain the agencies of different kinds of humans, on the one hand, and between human and nonhuman forms of agency, on the other" (Heise 2017: 6).

There may be yet a third conceptual tension having to do with how to define terms such as "human," "nonhuman," and "agency" in a historical perspective. How do the *anthropoi* of the Anthropocene differ from those of the premodern times? Can cultural memory still work as a foundational category of identity questions, as a form of orientation in space and time? Chakrabarty has his doubts, and his writings have indeed formulated a concern about history as a technique for making and negotiating meaning in the era of climate change. As Stephanie LeMenager puts it, "this scalar shift from the subject to the species could make history a largely irrelevant pursuit, as perhaps any moral or even ecological education might be in a world where the human is inscribed in stone" (2017: 473). I would argue that it is exactly at this point that some of the traditional tenets and key elements of a humanist education can come into play. As I have written elsewhere, the study of worlds far removed from our own is a highly relevant resource, because we can momentarily engage in an understanding of an alien world, establishing dialogues and making connections (Schliephake 2017a: 4). Questioning our past pathways taken and not taken in environmental and political terms is crucial in order "to understand the historical process, which has led homo sapiens in his path to the Anthropocene and how this has been shaped" (Cordovana & Chiai 2017: 11).

The "ecologization of history" does not have to be understood solely in material terms that look at environmental questions; rather, we have to realize that the ecological world is so intricately bound up with the world of culture that a loss in biodiversity actually coincides with cultural diversity loss, too (Mauelshagen 2016). Language is a case in point: on a global level, 34 percent of all languages are threatened (49). And, although the environmental humanities have a transnational outlook, it remains a problem that the field is dominated by the hegemonic language of English. "Monolingualism is currently one of (its) most serious intellectual limitations" (Heise 2006: 515), and the environmental humanities could benefit from a thorough historical reexamination of key terms inherited from antiquity, "culture" and "nature" being among the most prominent; word coinings ("ecology") also come to mind in this context.

Moreover, to quote LeMenager, "rethinking 'human tendency' ... still requires some slow reading, slow writing, and slow talk" (2017: 480). All learners of Latin, Greek, and other ancient languages will probably second this claim because old languages force us to slow down our reading habits, pondering meaning and intertextual connections. Again, I would say that this is a resource in its own right because it helps us think in long-term categories of cultural tradition and, for the lack of a better word, 'sustainability' (Schliephake 2017b). How the ancient cultures have managed to pass down knowledge through generation after generation is still a fascinating tale of the resilience of human meaning-making systems in the face of limited resources and adverse environmental conditions (after all, much of the reason why only a small percentage of ancient texts have come down to us has to do with environmental/climatic conditions). It is probably an even greater testament to their imaginative force and substantial knowledge that they can still inspire and fascinate generations of students today.

And, while we should "be wary of straightjacketing ancient Greco-Roman approaches and ethics into the terms of relatively recent debates, not only as historians but also as interested participants in contemporary debates about nature and value," as Brooke Holmes cautions, she also makes clear that "there is a risk, too, that in our enthusiasm for radical historicization we cut ourselves off from a 'premodern' past too abruptly, a risk felt all the more acutely as the horizon of interest in the past has moved steadily closer to the present" (Holmes 2014: 570). So, yes, the environmental humanities can benefit and learn from "ancient cultures." They are still fundamental repositories of knowledge, imagination, and cultural transformation. It is my hope that this Element will convince students and practitioners in the environmental humanities that this is truly the case. In order to achieve the desired effect, I opt for a methodology that could best be described as a dialectics of "distant" and "close" reading. It is distant in that it approaches the ancient world with the toolset of contemporary environmental theory; and it is close in that it tries to interpret the ancient texts and sources against their own respective cultural, religious, political, and social contexts.

Thus, Section 2 will make up the "distant" part, inquiring whether we can speak of an "ecological turn" in classical studies and developing models for further studies. In turn, Section 3 will engage in a close reading of the "storied ecologies" of the ancient world, discussing environmental theory and reconsidering the environmental aspects of mythology and religion with the help of classical Athens. Section 4 will present a synthesis of these two approaches and will discuss the role of ancient mythology in contemporary environmental theory. Because the ancient world is a rather vague term and encompasses so many different cultures, geographies, and time periods, my analysis cannot help but be fragmentary and necessarily incomplete (i.e. distant), but the overall narrative will try to closely follow some key motifs and stories that reverberated from the classical age all the way into imperial times and, eventually, to our own times.

2. The Ecological Turn in Classical Studies

Is there really an ecological turn in classical studies?

I do think that there is; and it has been going on for some time. But "ecology" is a somewhat misleading term in this context, because it can mean a lot of different things to different scholars (depending on their own approach and disciplinary background). Moreover, it does not always explicitly pop up as a concept in studies that nonetheless deal in subjects and sources whose main outlook would qualify as "ecological." To name just a few examples, landscape studies, studies of ancient Mediterranean economy and agriculture, resource use and colonization, *polis* and *chora*, medicine and the body, etc. most often have an outlook that at least takes environmental aspects into consideration. By now, there is also a vast body of work in ancient environmental history. In fact, this is a field where some major advances are to be expected in the next years due to new types of sources that are now being (re)considered and analyzed with scientific methods.

What I will, in the following, refer to as an "ecological turn" is an attempt, on my part, to come up with a synthesis of major approaches and trends that have substantially characterized some major works of classical studies in the last two decades. Firstly, I will define what I mean by ecology with the help of some definitions taken from biology, human ecology, geography, and history. Then, I want to discuss two different approaches to ecology and discuss their implications for the study of the ancient world: one that looks at the interplay between human systems and the nonhuman environment and one that starts from the observation that culture, too, can be compared to an ecological system and that takes myths and stories as integral parts of any human–"nature" interaction. This conceptualization of the ecological turn will provide the basis of the following sections and, hopefully, for an understanding of how integral the study of the classical world is to the interdisciplinary project of the environmental humanities.

Ecology and Ancient History

"Ecology" (a combination of Greek *oikos*, meaning "home" or "house(hold),'' and *logos*, meaning "reason" or "study") is not an ancient term. It was first coined by the zoologist Ernst Haeckel in 1866. Influenced by contemporary biologists as well as the writings of Alexander von Humboldt, which provided a synthesis of biology, geography, and meteorology to, for instance, discuss the growth of plants relative to their surroundings, the term became widely influential around the beginning of the twentieth century. Traditionally, it "has been defined as the study of the functional interrelationships of living organisms, played out on the stage of their inanimate surroundings" (Seidler & Bawa 2016: 71). It can be used to describe both the "organizational characteristics of a system" and the (teleological) "evolutionary pathways" found in "nature" (72).

Ecological thinking has, indeed, become integral to many challenges facing humankind on a global scale. During the second half of the twentieth century, it has increasingly entered the field of politics, but, in fact, it had characterized human–nature interactions from a very early time: "The urgent need to understand interactions between nature and human society is by no means new. Agriculture and animal husbandry have always demanded sophisticated awareness of the dynamics of social-ecological systems" (Seidler & Bawa 2016: 74). Although ecology is thus a modern term, it can nevertheless be used to analyze and describe premodern societies and how they depended on their natural environments while influencing them at the same time.

To any historian interested in ecological relationships in the past, this may be good news. It may be, however, complicated by the fact that ecology as a term poses a problem to traditional humanist approaches in so far as its nonanthropocentric outlook forces us to think in different terms and to take other factors into account than the traditional anthropogenic categories of meaning-making and decision-taking. In the life sciences, the term "ecosystem" refers to the totality of the relational structures between *all* living beings (Herrmann 2013: 85). Its central elements are made up of the community of life and the abiotic component of the biotope. Physical space, matter, and the diversity of biota combine to form a network connected through the energy flow of the food chain. Feedback effects between the individual components turn this network into a dynamic system with the ability for a certain degree of self-regulation and resilience in the face of outside influences.

In biology, there is a long tradition of stressing the way a given environment influences a single organism, but as Herrmann notes (2013: 87), a more synthetic approach, which gives more weight to the reciprocity between the entire ecosystem and its individual components, has recently gained widespread attention. As Lynn White Jr. already observed half a century ago, "all forms of life modify their contexts" (White Jr. 1967: 1203) – this is certainly the point where a truly historical perspective can enter ecological discussion, namely in assessing how humans, as part of the biosphere, have adapted to and transformed their respective environmental contexts. The relatively recent theory of "niche construction" helps render this historical perspective in biological terms. In short, niche construction is "the process whereby organisms, through their metabolism, their activities, and their choices, modify their own and/or each other's niches" (Odling-Smee 2003: 419). The term denotes activities of organisms that bring about changes in their environments, many of which are ecologically consequential.[5]

---

[5] I can only give a very succinct version of the theory, which has not gone unchallenged, especially by evolutionary biologists (cf. Scott-Phillips et al. 2014).

As Herrmann (2013: 87) argues, "culture" can be defined as the specific niche of humankind.[6] The niche of culture leads to and enables, according to Herrmann, fundamental changes of selective environmental parameters that have, in turn, consequences for humans and other organisms. Humans thus "construct" their own habitat to correspond to their own needs and with the instrumentalization of "natural" resources. While this process need not necessarily entail a specific teleological aim, it can have long-term effects on all forms of life in any given habitat. The domestication of certain types of plants and animals was such a major step, whereby the boundaries between culture and the ecosystem as a whole were transcended and, to echo Haber once again, the human "niche," enabling the active regulation and transformation of biological systems, led to the "ecological trap" of becoming dependent on a rather limited selection of plants and animals: "the transition from 'nature use' to 'land use'" entailed, in Haber's view, "a totally different way of treating the environment – indeed, from now on humans have been shaping their own environment at the cost of the environments of all other organisms on earth" (2007: 360).

This is, in my mind, an interesting take on an old problem, vexing both ecological science and environmental history for some time; namely, how to actually position humankind in the biosphere. As a distinct paradigm within history, environmental history owes a great deal to major implications of ecology. For, although its natural focus is the human, environmental history builds on the insight that "the human species is part of a community of life. It evolved within that community by competing against, cooperating with, imitating, using, and being used by other species" (Hughes 2016: 15). According to Donald Hughes, "What needs emphasis is that all human societies, everywhere, throughout history, have existed within and depended upon biotic communities" (15). So, while it is certainly important to stress the cultural specifications of the human niche within the ecosystem, it is equally vital – from a historical vantage point – to highlight how that niche, time and again, was an integral part of a material network with a resilience and agency of its own. It is only within such a framework that we stand a chance of developing historical models that take Val Plumwood's call for "ecological humanities" seriously by situating the human firmly within an environmental community and by showing how nonhumans were likewise integral to the cultural and, one might add, ethical niches created by humans (Plumwood 2002).

Based on an observation by E. O. Wilson (2004 [1978]), we can think of the human as dependent on an ecology shared with other nonhuman lifeforms and

---

[6] As Haber notes, it is, in ecological terms, not uncommon to speak of an "anthroposphere" as a separate part of the "biosphere" (Haber 2016: 19).

matter as well as on a culturally specific environment characterized by specific anthropogenic values and power relations (Haber 2016: 27). This is what Chakrabarty means when he claims that modern "science ... has doubled the figure of the human – you have to think of the two figures of the human simultaneously: the human-human and the non-human human" (Chakrabarty 2012: 11). This is also true for a historically deep perspective that traces the simultaneous and interrelated evolution of the natural and cultural ecosystems that have determined the course of premodern history. But this evolution was not a stable process, teleologically leading up to modernity; nor was it pre-determined due to specific, unchanging material frameworks. Rather, as the so-called "New Ecology" has shown, social-ecological systems have to be seen in a dynamic flux, with instabilities and disequilibria as permanently affecting the biophysical parameters of life.

According to the human geographer Karl Zimmerer, "Historical time with its emphasis on the irregular periodicity of environmental variations and ecological functioning has replaced the cyclical time of systems ecology," looking at "how the irregular temporal variation of ecological processes and so-called 'site histories' structure the foundations of environmental systems" (Zimmerer 1994: 110). It is within such a context, I would argue, that the "two figures of the human" come to the fore as both actively shaping and passively being shaped by environmental factors. This ecological outlook is a challenge to any anthropocentric model which claims that human agency alone has shaped the course of history, in fact problematizing what being "human" means and showing how our species is substantially interconnected with the world. In the words of Stacy Alaimo, "what was once the ostensibly bounded human subject enters a swirling landscape of uncertainty" (Alaimo 2012: 561).

One of the most influential works on premodern social-ecological history, entitled *The Corrupting Sea: A Study of Mediterranean History*, written by the medievalist Peregrine Horden as well as the ancient historian Nicholas Purcell and published in the year 2000, builds on some of the main premises connected to the "New Ecology" and synthetic ecosystems theory. In it, the authors opt for an approach they refer to as a "historical ecology," which "concerns itself with instability, disequilibria and chaotic fluctuations" (Horden & Purcell 2000: 49). They approach premodern environmental history as an intricate network of microecologies determined by shifting historical scenarios, local variations in space and biosphere, and cultural factors having to do with the stories and spirituality connected to certain landscapes. As they reflect on their use of the terminology of ecology and ecosystem-studies, it is "first and foremost a way of indicating that it is here a question of the many-faceted interactions between humanity and the environment, rather than of environmental primacy, of human autonomy, or of the limited responsiveness to surroundings implied by 'possibilism'" (45). They also make it clear that their approach is firmly grounded in history; that is, it gives prevalence to the study of cultural dynamics over ecological parameters. In the words of Horden and Purcell:

> The dynamics and flux of social allegiances and ordered behavior in the Mediterranean region will defy scientific modelling. Historical ecology, as opposed to other kinds, will therefore investigate these processes in a different spirit. The study of them may clearly be enhanced by frequent invocation of the natural ecologist's terms, procedures and self-reinventions. But without sustained attention to what is distinctively historical about the place of humanity within the environment, and particularly to the complexity of human interaction across large distances, the study of the Mediterranean past will ultimately not have advanced very far beyond Plato's simile of the frogs round the pond. (49)[7]

This approach has lastingly influenced many studies that have, since the new millennium, looked at different aspects of premodern environmental history and social-ecological relationships. Theirs is an ecological viewpoint in so far as it embeds human decision- and meaning-making in a complex web of social and natural factors. The "ecologization of history" can, in this context, be thought of as a reimagination of humanity's place in history, where its sociopolitical underpinnings are not separate but, rather, in constant exchange and interplay with natural history. In the following, I want to trace some of the major implications of these ecological approaches to classical times in order to see how they resonate with contemporary notions of human agency in the Anthropocene before moving on to discuss the resonating metaphor of storytelling and mythology as specific forms of cultural ecology.

"Ecologized History"

In the following, I want to give an outline of what I take as different, but interrelated, approaches to historical ecology in classical studies. I want to take up Garrard's dual project of "the historicization of ecology" and "the ecologization of history" alluded to earlier (Garrard 2014: 3–5). Differentiating between an "ecologized history" and a "storied ecology," I want to discuss two ways of studying ancient environments. While the former takes its main impetus from ecological models, and increasingly from scientific analysis, in order to gain a clearer picture of the overall material frameworks of

---

[7] The reference to Plato is a recurring image of how the ancient Greeks saw their own place in the Mediterranean. One section of the dialogue *Phaedo* reads: "We inhabit a small portion of the earth . . . living round the sea like ants and frogs round a pond" (Plato *Phaedo* 109B).

human–nature interactions in antiquity and how they evolved, the latter starts by reconsidering the environmental aspects of ancient texts and reconceptualizing mythological narratives, philosophical treatises, or epigraphic writings as sources that give a vivid account of how the ancients perceived, made sense of, or even protected their respective surroundings, negotiating ecological insights and wisdom in and through stories. Implicitly, these two approaches will also draw on two contemporary buzzwords associated with increasingly popularized forms of historiography, namely, "big history" and "deep history."

"Big" and "deep history" are concerned with long-term developments and universal patterns, including scales that encompass the cosmological. Where historiography has traditionally focused on a time frame starting in the "historical period," with a plethora of documentary and written evidence and with a particular emphasis on human civilization, both big and deep history are highly multidisciplinary in that they draw on recent scientific approaches to natural phenomena, embedding human history in an all-encompassing web of interaction with nonhuman forces and processes exceeding the narrow focus of anthropogenic cultural archives. But, where big history draws on a broad set of empirical data in order to explore cause-and-effect relations (Christian 2005), deep history has a narrower focus on humankind, tracing its evolution beyond what actually counts as prehistory and using advances in disciplines such as neurobiology or genetics (Smail 2008).

It should be clarified from the outset that I do not mean to suggest that either of the two approaches has made a lasting impact on classical studies – they have not, and, one might add, for good reason. Nonetheless, reflecting on their respective methodologies may, at least, be productive regarding some central concerns of contemporary historiography in the time of the Anthropocene with its characteristic merging of geohistory and human history. What I refer to as an "ecologized history" of the ancient world focuses on general patterns of the evolution of human systems and their interrelatedness with the nonhuman biophysical environments. It draws on an innovative array of new approaches such as palaeoclimatology and a set of quantifiable, statistical data.[8] A "storied ecology" perspective, on the other hand, is concerned with tracing human–"nature" interactions in the cultural archives of the ancient world. Drawing on the cognitive and emotional aspects related to storytelling, it investigates how cultural meaning-making is vital to social forms of landscape appropriation and the development of ecological knowledge.

---

[8] Other, recent approaches also include zooarchaeology (Monks 2017) and the "archaeology of human response," bringing disaster studies together with archaeology (Bawden & Reycraft 2000).

It should be made clear that both terms are to be understood not as labels actually used in ancient history or related disciplines but as attempts on my part to reflect on two distinct, yet interrelated, approaches to a historical ecology of the ancient world. In consequence, I use these terms with the intention of reflecting on the diverse paths an ecological turn in classical studies could take (or, rather, has already taken) and with the idea of drawing attention to how much these respective approaches can be read as a historical commentary on our own experiences in the Anthropocene. Nevertheless, ecologized history and storied ecology help resituate ancient environments within a debate in the humanities that has, for too long, narrowly focused on modernity.

We should probably begin by discussing the shapes an ecologized history of antiquity should not take. A comparison with big history is inevitable at this point: the latter approach hardly shies away from drawing broad connections between the modern world and antiquity, often presenting the two as being situated in a line of continuity where recent developments stand in for or are modelled upon analogous ancient experiences. Connected to this is a tendency of arguing for the epoch-spanning universality or recurrence of certain systemic characteristics and events. Depending on the sets of data and theoretical models used, there is nothing inherently wrong with such an approach. It may be an attempt on the part of some scholars to argue for the relevance of the discipline and show how vital the ancient world still is for an understanding of our own present – this is, in fact, also one of the aims of this Element. However, drawing big connecting links and analogies between antiquity and modernity can some-times be taken a step too far.

One of the most prominent examples of big history with a classical bent can be found in the works of Stanford archaeologist Ian Morris. His recent book *Foragers, Farmers, and Fossil Fuels: How Human Values Evolve* (2015), which stems from his Tanner Lectures held in 2012, and which includes highly engaged responses by the classicist Richard Seaford, the sinologist Jonathan D. Spence, the philosopher Christine M. Korsgaard, and the acclaimed novelist Margaret Atwood, presents a macro-historical take on the evolution of human values in three successive stages of development. Morris' overall thesis is that social forms of organization and their prevailing values are dependent upon and change according to the different modes of energy capture alluded to in the book's title.

Morris makes use of a functionalist approach that shows how values are shaped by the respective needs of a given historical society, which are directly related to energy extraction and social forms of resource management. Morris harks back to an exclusively anthropocentric perspective. Integrating the human within a biotic community, or granting that community a place inside the cultural norms and values so central to the book's outlook, is not even an option for Morris. Interestingly enough, the term "ecology" hardly makes an appearance in the text, although the book draws to a great extent on insights and material taken from, for instance, population ecology.

The reason why I still include Morris' study in these considerations is not due to the popular nature of his arguments but, rather, because its main implications actually stand, at least in my mind, in the way of truly historical-ecological thinking. For instance, Morris, who counts himself, in the terms of Max Weber, among the "explainers" as opposed to the "understanders" of historical contingency and development, writes in his introduction:

> Explainers need to complement the hundreds of thick descriptions of meaning in specific cultures with broad comparisons spanning large areas and long periods of time. These will be thin descriptions, largely (though not exclusively) quantitative, and not very participatory. They will be coarse-grained, because they sweep up into a single story of hundreds of societies, thousands of years, and millions of people, and reductionist, because they seek answers by boiling down the teeming variety of lived experience to simpler underlying principles. (Morris 2015: 8–9)

This reasoning may be in line with some of the tenets characteristic of the zeitgeist of the Anthropocene outlined earlier. It could even help in discerning some general developments that have led to our presumed ecological crisis, but, from a historical-ecological vantage point, its perspective and implications are various scales too big. The problem with such an approach is not only its reductionism – a fact Morris is well aware of – but, rather, that it completely blanks out the particularities and lived realities that have determined, time and again, the interconnections between societies and their nonhuman biophysical surroundings. From an ecological perspective alone, what Morris terms "simpler underlying principles" are, in fact, complex feedback systems in constant fluctuation and change. In the *longue durée*, there may be some overarching principles having to do with material and climatic frameworks, but big data analysis alone will not do if we want to arrive at an analysis that takes human and natural systems as co-constituting factors of historical ecology.[9]

---

[9] A second example that is not as much a big history, but draws on some of the premises also found in Morris' approach, is the important monograph study, *The Rise and Fall of Classical Greece* (2015), written by one of the foremost experts in the ancient Greek world, Josiah Ober (like Morris, a Stanford scholar). The book analyzes the "causal relationship between political and economic development" (xv). Its central argument is that growth in the political, or rather *polis*, ecology of the Greek world with its 1,000 independent cities (plural: *poleis*) created robust conditions for real economic growth from the eighth century BCE onwards. Like Morris, Ober draws on a set of big data to prove his argument, also using recent theoretical models like New Institutional Economics and the work of North et al. (2009). Yet, as reviewers have noted, neither the data nor the model as such can fully convince because they are highly selective and ignore the

There are data sets that look promising for an ecologized history of the ancient world, and it may very well be the case that a closer dialogue between ancient history and natural science will garner promising new insights in the forthcoming years, possibly strengthening the impact that the study of ancient environments can have on contemporary interdisciplinary debates in the environmental humanities. Historical climatology and palaeoclimatology have come to the fore in recent times as approaches that, with innovative methodologies and rigorous scientific testing, have created a pool of complicated data that will certainly provide further insights into ancient social structures and how they related to experience of climate shocks. As J. G. Manning has recently argued, "The challenge for ancient historians is to build more complex social models" (2018: 136) based on such work. However, this also brings some methodological problems, because these data sets both imply uncertainties about the biophysical impacts of climate change in history and do not automatically correlate with social change. "The usual assumption that changes in climate regime drove social changes is certainly too simplistic," cautions Manning, and adds that "we should think about climate and climate change inputs as components of coupled human-natural system" (136). This is an important insight for creating a historical ecology of antiquity in so far as it focuses on coupled feedback systems between humans and their respective environments and because it helps undermine environmental determinism by giving precedence to the adaptive capacities and scales of resilience of both human societies and ecosystems alike (137).

In his own work, Manning has especially focused on the ancient economy as well as on the development of models that help "understand the complexities of premodern societies by adding environmental constraints and shocks as an additional component to coupled human-natural system dynamics" (141). For instance, by bringing different types of proxy data (from pollen analysis and lake sediments to ice core records) together with written historical sources, Manning has argued that datable volcanic eruptions in different parts of the world had measurable climatic effects that time and again perturbed the Nile flow. In the Hellenistic period (ca. 323–30 BCE), for example, Manning suggests that "the sequence of eruptions we observe . . . may have had impacts in four related areas: (1) agricultural production, (2) food supply, (3) social unrest, and (4) disease" (161).

However, Manning does not replace an older form of environmental determinism with a new one by bringing climatic factors into play; rather, he opts for a relational, dynamic model that "seek[s] multicausal explanations for human

---

contingent factors and many contexts of the political economy of the greater Mediterranean world, within which the development of the political economy of the Greek *poleis* evolved.

responses and social change" (147). This is one of the tasks (and challenges) awaiting any ecologized history of the ancient world. It is timely not only in that it integrates new scientific data and looks at "climate change" as a significant factor in history (Harris 2013; Bresson 2014) but also in that it oftentimes gives prevalence to source material taken from the nonhuman world. Needless to say, these sources are analyzed with the help of anthropogenic technology and from an anthropocentric vantage point, but it still takes the "natural" world and the history it tells seriously as either driving or interacting with human systems.

Conceptually, the project of an ecologized history can be brought together with a point Richard Kerridge has recently made with regard to the Anthropocene and its related terminology in humanistic studies. Using the metaphor of "zooming in" and "zooming out," Kerridge argues that the Anthropocene demands a dual approach: "the necessary zooming involves withdrawing to the point from which humanity is visible as a single geomorphic force, and then zooming back in, perhaps further than before, to make necessary distinctions between rich and poor, privileged and oppressed" (2017: xvii). The same could be said regarding an ecologized history: it needs a zooming out that takes natural forces and their feedback relations with human societies into account as integral parts of history, and it needs a zooming in to analyze what kind of effects these overarching biophysical and material frameworks had on the structure of a society. In historical terms, the farthest one can zoom out in a chronological sense is probably to about 12,000 years ago, when the climate entered the modern interglacial warm period known as the Holocene. Arguably, this was the backdrop to the most significant shifts in human history; namely, the rise of agriculture and complex political structures. But it was also a time that itself was characterized by climate change on different scales.

As Kyle Harper has shown in his monograph *The Fate of Rome: Climate, Disease, and the End of an Empire* (2017), the Roman Empire "reached its maximal extent and prosperity in the folds of a late Holocene climate period called the Roman Climate Optimum (RCO)" (14). As Harper's study illustrates,

> the climate regime was a silent, cooperative force in the seemingly virtuous circle of empire and prosperity," but it was also "by turns subtle and over-whelming, alternatingly constructive and destructive. . . . (C)limate change was always an *exogenous* factor, a true wild card transcending all the other rules of the game. From without, it reshaped the demographic and agrarian foundations of life, upon which the more elaborate structures of society and state depended (15; emphasis in original)

Harper does not make the mistake of drawing too many parallels to our own ecological crises and, more importantly, to contemporary anthropogenic climate change. Rather, he, too, is concerned with integrating the nonhuman world firmly into the bigger picture of ancient history, instead of taking it, as older approaches had done, as "a static backdrop" (290).

Harper paints a complex picture that involves many nonhuman agents in the shaping and eventual transformation of the Roman Empire in Late Antiquity. And, while Harper perceives these phenomena from the vantage point of the many written sources analyzed in his book, he still closes with a poignant observation that shows how far big ecological takes on the ancient world inevitably serve as "a mirror and a measure"; as, in fact, being "part of an ongoing story" (292). "The long, intertwined story of humanity and nature is full of paradox, surprise, and blind chance," writes Harper. "That is why the particularity of history matters. Nature, like humanity, is cunning, but constrained by the circumstances of the past. Our story, and the story of the planet, are inseparable" (292).

Thus, this ecologized history helps, in one way, to answer the question posed at the outset: does the ancient *anthropos* have a place in the Anthropocene? Yes and No. No, because there are many modern environmental and climatic effects that are anthropogenic in kind and that do not have an ancient equivalent – despite the observation that there are levels of heavy metal pollution visible in the Greenland ice caps from the time of the early and middle Roman Empire that were not again reached until the eighteenth and nineteenth centuries, i.e. the beginnings of the Industrial Revolution (Langin 2018). Yes, because it shows how far the ancient world had already been caught up in environmental conditions that lastingly influenced patterns of cultural meaning-making, social organization, and resilience. And these show that there are, indeed, connecting links that can be drawn between our own times and antiquity, especially when we take into account the many nonhuman agents embedded in environmental feedback systems.

For Harper, they come in the form of "germs" as "unruly and decisive facts of history" (Harper 2017: 16). Accordingly, he invites an altogether different perception of the "Roman world ... as an ecological context for microorganisms" (17). But, as he shows, these microorganisms did not only have an agency of their own; there was also an interdependency between how the Roman Empire organized itself structurally and the environmental threats (including disease) to which it became vulnerable. The dense urban settlements are a case in point, just like the processes of landscape transformation, time and again giving way to an anthropogenic fantasy of a mastery over "nature" while, in fact, becoming ever more open to unforeseen ecological change.

This ecologized history of the ancient world is new. It is reflective of an insight summed up by Linda Nash: "Humans – and many animals – grow up in environments furnished by the work of previous generations, and as they grow they come to carry certain forms within their bodies – specific skills, sensibilities, and dispositions – that emerge in response to those constructed environments" (Nash 2017: 407). As she continues, "the essential role of changing historical environments" consists not only "in constraining and enabling social organization, but also in making us who we are both biologically and socially, undergirding our intellect and culture, and shaping our development over the scale of both individual lives and generations" (408).

This is true of the ancient world as much as it is true of our own. To a certain degree, we all stand in an intellectual and cultural tradition with the ancients; they still shape how we script and understand the "human" place in the world. But that is only one side of the story. Contemporary experiences unconsciously shape how we perceive the past; they open up new historical models to frame social change and meaning. The ecologized history of antiquity is, in other words, of our own making. It is reflective of our concerns and poignant insights in the Anthropocene. And it is reflective of a paradox engrained in any historical ecology: on the one hand, "the history of both human culture and the human body is, must be, environmental through and through" (Nash 2017: 411), but, on the other hand, "any environmental history must confront the idea that the environment about which we write is, inevitably, something that we always understand through language and certain cultural practices" (Nash 2006: 10). And it is this latter aspect of the equation that we will turn to in the next paragraph.

"Storied Ecology"

As already outlined, a storied ecology of the ancient world is concerned with the study of human thought and meaning-making connected to the natural environment and attitudes toward it, including proto-ecological systems of inquiry as well as religions, philosophies, and political ideologies. There is a vast body of literature on what could be described as environmental theories in Greco-Roman antiquity. Both Don Hughes (1994, 2014) and Lukas Thommen (2012) have, in their influential and important environmental histories of the ancient world, dedicated long passages to how the ancient Greeks and Romans perceived their natural surroundings, how they reflected on humanity's place in the world, and how they experienced phenomena like pollution.

There are also a number of studies that have dealt with the question of whether there was something akin to "ecological" thought in Greco-Roman antiquity (Rackham 1996; Vögler 2000; Thommen 2011; Egerton 2012; Irby et al. 2016). All of these studies have value in themselves, and they have explored the question in great depth and clarity, often drawing on source material that starts with the so-called Ionian or Pre-Socratic philosophers and leads to the classical *polis* and the writings of Aristotle and Theophrastus and, at least in some cases, to the "Second Sophistic" and late antique philosophy. After all, the fundamentals of ancient philosophy are particularly relevant not only because they formulated the first concepts of an order and stability in nature and debated ideas of ascesis or autarky, which still figure prominently in environmental debates, but also because they reflected on evolutionary patterns and the entanglement of mind and matter. When I choose not to go down that same track at this point, this is not because I think that everything has been said about the subject or because I do not want to discuss the same material all over again. In fact, I continue my "distant reading" exactly for the reason that I actually do think that more could be said about ecological awareness in antiquity and because I am convinced that it still has some powerful implications for our own times.

It should be clear by now that ecology is a complex notion, the more so if the term is applied to societies who, strictly speaking, did not know science in our sense of the term and where the nature–culture binary (if it existed at all) did not carry the heavy onto-epistemological and ethical baggage that it does today. As Oliver Rackham puts it, there is a danger that one may create what he terms a "pseudo-ecology" of premodernity, for instance by "confusing ecology with the environment: to treat living creatures as part of the scenery of the theatre, rather than as actors in the play. Plants and animals are not generalized nature, not the passive recipients of whatever mankind chooses to inflict on them: they are thousands of individual species, each with its own behavior which has to be understood" (Rackham 1996: 17).[10] This is an important observation, but his remarks reach more deeply, not only because he criticizes an approach that merely uses the label "ecology" without bringing the nonhuman environment and other species center stage in the historical analysis but also because Rackham holds that there is a danger of anachronism, "geographical over-generalization," and a misguided preoccupation with "ancient *attitudes* to nature": "The history of nature is not the same as the history of the things that people have *said* about nature" (17; emphasis in original).

This statement, again, brings to the fore the difficulties involved in the project of coming up with a historical ecology of the ancient world. On the one hand, we have to rely on ancient texts and interpretations, and on the other, we have to be constantly aware of their own limitations. The terms "ecologized history" and "storied ecology" are certainly related, but they should also point to the divide

---

[10] One might even add that, in the context of a historical ecology of antiquity, the hyphen "Greco-Roman" is misleading because both "cultures display marked ecological differences" (Foxhall et al. 2007: 92).

that still exists between material approaches relying on quantifiable data and textual modes of inquiry. Perhaps the limits to a historical understanding of ecology have to do with our own general outlook on ecological issues and certain limits on truly perceiving the community of life as an interrelated system.

When I still speak of a storied ecology, I do so in the full awareness that this outlook, too, has its limits when trying to account for environmental perception and knowledge in antiquity. In the strict sense of the term, it is not really an ecology at all, because I use it in the metaphorical way of reflecting on how the interconnection between human systems and their natural surroundings found an imaginative echo chamber in the works of culture and meaning-making, where it still resonates today. This is actually an old approach with a long tradition. In his multivolume bestseller *Kosmos*, Alexander von Humboldt already came up with a holistic take on culture–nature interaction, in fact, perceiving "human responses to nature as themselves natural phenomena" (Jenkins 2007: 90). The geographer Clarence Glacken took up this approach in the twentieth century in his monograph study *Traces on the Rhodian Shore* (1967), which paints an impressive tapestry of premodern views of the environment. Both Humboldt and Glacken understood the importance of the environmental imagination for how societies draw deep connections to their habitats, how they reflect on imbalances in the social-natural dynamics of ecosystems, and how they incite emotional and cognitive processes that can have practical effects upon how communities engage with their material environments.

Some of the insights and research approaches that today are being referred to as the environmental humanities were thus, in a way, also anticipated and modeled in older studies of premodern culture. What makes a storied ecology of the ancient world "deep" in the first place is both its chronological scope, tracing ideas and cultural imaginations of the environment down to the earliest written sources in antiquity, and its insistence on the codependency of natural processes and cultural forms of meaning-making, forms that have, time and again, reached out to the material world, symbolically appropriating it in and through language. Such a storied ecology takes every possible textual and visual remnant of the past as a possible source for an inquiry into environmental interrelations – not solely those that obviously have a "(pseudo)-ecological" outlook.

In its metaphorical usage of the term, a storied ecology builds and expands on a major sub-strand of contemporary environmental theory. As the anthropologist, semiotician, and cyberneticist Gregory Bateson once observed, ecological thinking is closer to metaphoric than to logocentric speech (Bateson 1991). Bateson himself formulated a complex theory of what he referred to as an "ecology of mind" or "ecology of ideas" from the 1940s up to the 1970s. It was based on the premise that there exist complex feedback systems between mind and body, culture and nature. Describing them as the "patterns that connect" (Bateson 2002[1972]: 7), Bateson holds that they make up intersubjective communication circuits between the "total interconnected social system and planetary ecology" (Bateson 2000: 467). Hence, culture is the stage where this interconnectivity between humans and their surrounding ecosystems is put center stage.

A storied ecology is fundamentally connected both to the interrelationship between culture and nature, made visible in human meaning-making systems, and to a history of ideas and its ecological implications. As Bateson claims, "the very meaning of 'survival' becomes different when we stop talking about the survival of something bounded by the skin and start to think of the survival of the system of ideas in circuit." This is exactly for the reason that, as an individual living being, everyone dies; but "the ideas, under further transformation, may go on out in the world in books or works of art." Thus, for instance, "Socrates, as a bioenergetic individual, is dead. But much of him still lives as a component in the contemporary ecology of ideas" (Bateson 2000: 467). This is a powerful metaphor for processes of classical reception that have, in a long history of ideas and cultural transmission, instrumentalized and transformed ancient culture. It also helps render the *longue durée* of cultural processes of adaption to and interaction with contexts that include the nonhuman world.

The anthropologist Julian Steward, who was influenced by Bateson and Franz Boas (a devoted disciple of Alexander von Humboldt), thus coined the term "cultural ecology" to underline that ecology is also useful for the analysis of culture. Steward used the expression mainly in the sense of analyzing how humans adapt to their biophysical environments and how that adaption propels culture change (1972[1955]). "Culture" encompasses the knowledge, practices, and technologies that have historically been shaped by preceding generations and that people have adopted as fundamental aspects of their own lives. Although the theory implies the possibility of environmental determinism over human actions – one paradigm within an "ecology of ideas" where ancient thought is still very prevalent (Kennedy & Jones-Lewis 2015) – it is also based on the premise that the evolution of nature and culture work separately from one another.

For instance, Finke's "evolutionary cultural ecology" recognizes the relative independence and self-reflexive dynamics of cultural processes. In his view, information and communication have become major driving forces of human ecosystems. Especially, language represents a "missing link" between cultural and natural evolution (Finke 2006) because it not only relates back to concrete biophysical forms of information and communication in the pre-cultural world of nature but also transforms them into more abstract, symbolic, and generalizing systems of human interpretation and self-interpretation. To take up the concept of the cultural niche again, the characteristic environments of humans are not just external biophysical systems but internal "landscapes of the mind" (Zapf 2017: 65).

This is also what the term "storied ecology" implies: it is a way of uncovering the culturally coded and symbolically significant "landscapes of the mind" that appear in ancient texts. A storied ecology of ancient culture, in a way, builds on an important insight by Hubert Zapf, namely that "in its aesthetic transformation of experience, literature acts like an ecological force within the larger system of cultural discourse and knowledge. . . . From its beginnings in storytelling and oral narratives, . . . literature has symbolically expressed the fundamental interconnectedness between culture and nature in tales of human genesis, of metamorphosis, of symbiotic co-evolution between different life forms" (Zapf 2017: 65).

This is not to say that we should put all source criticism and contextualization aside and engage in some transcendent, even esoteric reading that reaffirms a romanticized notion and, one might add, ahistorical version of ancient culture. Quite the contrary: I would argue that such an insight can actually inspire an alternative reading practice that looks for cultural ecological implications in and between texts that are, to the naked eye, not environmentally related at all. It also means reconsidering the role of nonhuman nature and "companion species" (Haraway 2003) in ancient texts, not solely as a backdrop to human actions and decisions but as constitutive factors of what Westling has referred to as the "human-animal dance" (2006: 11), a closeness between humans and nonhumans that can be found in all ancient literary genres, from archaic epic to Roman funerary steles.

The copresence of nonhuman forms of life is an important aspect in this context because it has challenged conceptions of the human from the earliest written sources onward. Animals played an important role as "companions" (Haraway 2003), but they were also made the subject of systemic violence (Kalof 2007) – indeed, so much so that some species, like the mountain lion, had become extinct in Europe by the end of antiquity. Thus, human-driven extinction as one of the key features of the Anthropocene had been prefigured in ancient times. A storied ecology can help in illustrating the complex ecological interactions between humans and animals that characterized ancient life – and, although I will not do so in this Element, it should be noted that this is a field of inquiry where more could be done.

I do not mean to suggest that we should all follow the path of storied ecology. But I do think that this theory harbors a lot of potential and can complement a lot of existing work, especially where cognitive approaches to ancient myth, landscapes, and environmental knowledge are concerned. These are all subjects that have yielded fascinating studies over the last decades. In a remarkable essay, Esther Eidinow proposed that myths and the process of myth-making, understood as "conscious narratives that are told and retold" by a society in order to understand their surroundings, can be seen as cultural forms that contain ecological knowledge and that transmit this knowledge down generational lines (Eidinow 2016: 48). Drawing on two interrelated Aristotelian concepts of knowledge, *sophia* (here understood as "theoretical wisdom") and *phronesis* (translated as "practical wisdom"), Eidinow shows how myths are an imaginative space for bringing together environmental and social modes of knowledge. She draws on an array of examples that demonstrate how myths were, for instance, used to reflect on the close ties between communities and the landscapes in which they settled.

This observation is based on a long line of inquiry in classical studies that has demonstrated how myths "(illustrate) an intricate, integral relationship with its physical surroundings" (Hawes 2017: 1). For instance, as Hawes puts (their), "We find nymphs transformed into trees and springs; rivers at once gods and forces of nature; tombs marking the burial sites of heroes; place names explained by the deeds of their eponyms" (1). This is because "stories articulate a particular kind of conceptual map" and "storytelling" is a cultural "activity which is both precisely situated in, and contingent on, the environment" (1).[11] Rather than presenting a fantastic realm with archetypal figures situated in a distant past and far-off place, myth is, according to this concept, intricately bound up with spatial thinking. It is an avenue into showing the inherent dynamic and local variations that had diverse impacts on a shared cultural code.

Reconceptualizing myths as "stories," Johnston has recently argued that myths make up a narrative cultural reservoir that is an integral part of what we term the adaptive and resilient character of societies, because "they are especially good at describing events that have not been experienced by either the narrators or the listeners themselves so persuasively that those events become credible, thus enlarging the audience's sense of what *might* be possible" (Johnston 2018: 10; emphasis in original). In this context, we might think of the

---

[11] As Christina A. Salowey has illustrated with the help of a close reading of "river scenes" in ancient epic, "the volatile actions of the mythic rivers are consistent with a specific set of Mediterranean geomorphological characteristics that dictated the behaviour and management of watercourses" (2017: 161). One example would be the River Scamander in the entire twenty-first book of Homer's *Iliad*. On this, see also Holmes (2015).

well-known example of Odysseus' adventures. His journey does not follow any known itinerary, and it includes many fantastical elements. Still, it would help Greek speakers to literally navigate the imaginary border zones between their own world and what lay beyond. Odysseus' description of the island of the Cyclopes is a prime example of the contact between civilized man and wild nature (Homer Odyssey 9, 106–115), and it could serve a proto-colonial discourse in a time characterized by increased mobility (Schliephake 2019).

These two traits now associated with myth, that is, how they contain environmental knowledge and how they transform this knowledge into the de-pragmatized story mode, show how integral myths were for the storied ecologies of the ancient world. With their affecting and emotional qualities, they reached a wide audience, and, what is more, they inspired action (Eidinow 2016: 49–50; Johnston 2018). They were, in other words, integral to the cultural ecology, functioning both as transmitters of knowledge and as a medium in which this knowledge could be imaginatively tested, transformed, and finally adapted to changing sociopolitical or environmental contexts. As recent studies in cognition have shown, "the sphere of generating knowledge is situated in a bodily matrix, and consists of interactive data processing systems . . .. Cognition is inseparable from bodily actions, through necessary sensory inputs. Human cognition is also governed by human biological endowments which find expression within a social milieu" (Hassan 2004: 315). "Communication" as a central medium for the "flow of knowledge and beliefs" (315) is a central cognitive and, one might add, evolutionary capacity of humankind. It is a way of reaching out, not only beyond the individual body but also beyond the boundaries of one's society, to other cultures and also to the nonhuman world.

Nonetheless, we should not lose sight of the power structures, asymmetries, and hierarchies engrained in this exchange. More often than not, myths and stories were used to make manifest political claims of authority and leadership; they were integral to identity (Gehrke 1994) and thus also to processes of exclusion and exploitation (of both landscape and people). We should thus be wary of mistaking a storied ecology for an idyllic or harmonious representation of the relationship between landscape/environment and people/society. In a historical sense, this approach is most productive, I would argue, when we take seriously the ecological aspects of the stories that ancient societies told of their world while also considering how far these natural-cultural (Haraway 2003) assemblages were also instruments of ideology and violence.

Only then will it be truly possible to integrate a storied ecology into ancient history. A historical ecology works best when we can show, on the one hand, how the environments in which the ancients lived were socioculturally con-structed in and through stories and, on the other hand, how the biophysical surroundings were integrated, not solely as a backdrop but as agents, into these stories; how, in other words, the nonhuman world became a constitutive factor of the cultural processes of meaning-making and the symbolical articulation of future or alternative worlds – and thus vital for the survival of cultural systems of thought in the face of various detrimental political and/or environmental factors of change.

In order to discuss some of the implications of an ecologized history and storied ecology for classical studies, I want to engage in a close reading in the following section. So, whereas the previous half of this Element was distant in scope and outlook, the second half will be concerned with creating a closer dialogue between ancient material and modern environmental theory. In the following section, the starting point will be classical Athens, which we will visit with some key theoretical notions of current debates in the environmental humanities. The aim is to test some of the presuppositions formulated regarding an ecologized history and a storied ecology and to clear the path for further research and dialogue between the ancient and the modern world.

3. Athena and the Olive: Environmental Aspects of Ancient Greek Religion Revisited

Did ancient (olive) trees have standing?

This question is a variation on Christopher D. Stone's landmark monography *Should Trees Have Standing? Law, Morality, and the Environment* (2010 [1972]). Stone's book was a rallying point for the environmental movement and stands as one of the most important environment-related texts of the second half of the twentieth century. It made the case for why natural objects should have legal rights, so that nonhuman animals and plants are protected for future generations.

Although the question may seem strange in the context of antiquity – to my knowledge, such an issue was never seriously disputed in any legal setting and would, in all likelihood, not have made much sense to anyone in the ancient world – it was, nevertheless, as I want to argue, a question that ancient societies actually posed themselves, if only implicitly and in a different context from what we would probably suspect. As I want to show, it was present in myth, cult, and sacred law – in other words, in ancient religion.

Ancient religion has often been studied with regard to its environmental aspects. There is a plethora of studies that have looked at how gods and heroes embodied qualities of natural forces (Trépanier 2010; Scheer 2019), how the mythological stories turned the natural environment with its groves, grottoes, and springs into what Kate Rigby has once referred to, in a different context, as a "topography of the sacred" (2004), how divination, especially sacrifice, negotiated the boundaries between human and animal, etc. These are all still highly relevant issues, and I will, in the following, refer to some major scholarly paradigms and key studies. But this is not my main topic.

What I want to look at is how the storied ecology of ancient Greek religion was part of an all-encompassing ecology situated at the intersecting lines between human community and natural environment. I want to ask what kind of ecological understanding and knowledge mythological stories entailed, and I want to illustrate how this knowledge found its concrete manifestation in civic identity, economy, and law. Thereby, I take the storied ecology of Greek religion not so much as a symbolical realm, loaded with archetypal figures, but rather as the concrete, narrative manifestation of a highly dynamic, material environment. "Religion" is a complicated term in this context; in fact, so complex that a longer discussion would far exceed the narrow confines of this Element. For the sake of brevity, I understand religion as a combination of beliefs, narratives, and practices that, depending on the situation, involve agents that are, in one way or another, nonhuman and superior (Rüpke 2016: 19).[12]

In the following, I want to revisit one of the most famous of all Athenian stories, the contest between Athena and Poseidon, analyzing its storied ecology and how it connected to the ecology of arboriculture and its political significance in ancient society, revisiting an old subject with some key theoretical notions of the environmental humanities.

The Contest between Athena and Poseidon – a Storied Ecology

One of the quintessential classical myths was the story of the contest between Athena and Poseidon for control of Athens and Attica. The many sources in extant written sources illustrate the popularity and the dynamic character of the mythological tale,[13] with various reliefs and vase paintings attesting to its highly imaginative and attractive quality for visual artists (Marx 2011:

---

[12] The question of what religion is, and what functions it serves, has been widely debated over the last decades. Introductions into the field often note that Greeks lacked an equivalent word, but that does not mean that ancient Greeks lacked religion. Many approaches are functionalist in that they show how Greek religion was embedded in social and political institutions and helped strengthen social identity and community cohesion. There are also approaches that highlight the individual aspects of religious "belief" and how, as a cultural phenomenon, religion is tied in with human cognition and individual minds. Excellent introductions into the debate can be found in Larson (2016), Kindt (2012), and Rosenberger (2012) with a comparison between Greek and Roman religion.

[13] Euripides *Ion* 1433–1436; Euripides *The Trojan Women* 799–803; Xenophon *Memorabilia* 3,5,10; Isocrates *Panathenaicus* 193; Ovid *Metamorphoses* 6,70–82; Hyginus *Fabulae* 164; Callimachus *Iambi* 4,67–69, Varro *Fragmenta* 11.

33–37). In the mythological textbook of Apollodorus (*Bibliotheca* 3,14) we find one of the longest versions:

> Cecrops, son of the soil, with a body compounded of man and serpent, was the first king of Attica, and the country which was formerly called Acte he named Cecropia after himself. In his time, they say, the gods resolved to take possession of cities in which each of them should receive his own peculiar worship. So Poseidon was the first that came to Attica, and with a blow of his trident on the middle of the acropolis, he produced a sea which they now call Erechtheis. After him came Athena, and, having called on Cecrops to witness her act of taking possession, she planted an olive tree, which is still shown in the Pandrosium. But when the two strove for possession of the country, Zeus parted them and appointed arbiters, not, as some have affirmed, Cecrops and Cranaus, not yet Erysichthon, but the twelve gods. And in accordance with their verdict the country was adjudged to Athena, because Cecrops bore witness that she had been the first to plant the olive. (transl. J. G. Frazer 2016 [1921])

(Pseudo-)Apollodorus' account is replete with some variations, typical of Greek myths. Other accounts differ on the nature of the judges, whether they were gods or humans (with class and gender differences as important categories and, eventually, decisive factors) (Himerius 6,7–8; Augustine *De Civitate Dei* 18,9),[14] and what the winning criterion was – the first to arrive in a race from Mt. Olympos, the value of the gift to the city, the power of the token, or the call upon a witness (or the failure to do so).[15] There is no question that Athena and Poseidon are the central protagonists of the story, that their contest takes place on the Acropolis, and that Athena plants the very first olive tree (Patay-Horváth 2015: 353–354). The story symbolizes *agon*, contest or struggle, introducing it as a central piece in how the Acropolis became what we might call a "storied place": "The agon is one of Athena's many fields of operation, her sacred olive

---

[14] The Roman Marcus Varro (quoted in Augustine *De Civitate Dei* 18,9) recounts the myth with a strong focus on the Athenian democratic institution of direct vote and gender aspects of civic life: "Cecrops convoked all the citizens of either sex to give their vote, for it was then the custom in those parts for the women also to take part in public deliberations. When the multitude was consulted, the men gave their votes for Neptune (i.e. Poseidon), the women for Minerva (i.e. Athena); and as the women had a majority of one, Minerva conquered. Then Neptune, being enraged, laid waste to the lands of the Athenians, by casting up the waves of the sea; for the demons have no difficulty in scattering any waters more widely. The same authority said, that to appease his wrath the women should be visited by the Athenians with the three-fold punishment – that they should no longer have any vote; that none of their children should be called after their mothers; and that no one should call them Athenians" (transl. Dods et al. 1948). On the containment of the female or gendered qualities associated with women in myth and the sculptures of the Parthenon, see Castriota (1992: 145–151).

[15] The contest continued genealogically: Later Poseidon's son Eumpolos made war on Athens to avenge his father's defeat and was killed by Erechtheus, who was killed by Poseidon. Cf. Euripides *Erechtheus* (Collard & Cropp 2008); Isocrates *Panathenaicus* 193.

tree, the tangible sign of her defeat of Poseidon, was not only the Acropolis' first victory monument but was also, according to tradition, the mythical first olive tree, the one that engendered all others ..." (Hurwit 1999: 231).

In the Greek tradition, Poseidon's present for the later Athenians is usually referred to as the *Thalassa Erechtheis* (the sea of Erechtheus); in Roman tradition there is also talk of a horse (Servius on Vergil *Georgics* 1,12). In fact, the motif of Poseidon contesting for a city with a respective patron deity is a recurring element of foundational or, rather, "prefoundational" (Berman 2017) myths of different *poleis* in the ancient world (Parker 1987: 199; Meyer 2017: 395–397). Read environmentally, the narrative containment of the fearsome aspects of Poseidon as a sender of storms and earthquakes was central to these stories. In Athens, where the scene found one prominent expression on the west pediment of the Parthenon,[16] Poseidon was an important god, connected to civic identity due to his help in the sea battle against the Persians at Salamis (480 BCE), and highly symbolic of Athens' rise to a naval power in the aftermath of the Persian Wars.

The invocation of the hybrid, semi-anthropomorphized figure of Kekrops, miraculously born from the ground, points to the fact that there had been a settlement on the Acropolis prior to the arrival of the two gods. His serpent-like character and the setting also bring to mind the Python at the oracle site of Delphi (Elderkin 1941: 117). We do have plenty of evidence that the Athenian Acropolis had been settled during the Bronze Age, with a remarkable continuity to the classical age, and the prominent role of water in the myth may attest to long oral traditions attached to the seepage of water at the southwest corner of the present Erechtheion or the underground passage to a spring known since Mycenaean times (118). The story, however, also ties in with the rather peculiar Athenian origin story: in classical times, Athenians claimed autochthony; that is, they believed or, rather, proclaimed that their ancestors were born from the soil of Attica (Clements 2015). The myth explains the aetiology of "Athens" and describes the close relationship between the city and the goddess as well as between the city and the olive tree.[17]

Traditionally, the story of the contest has been brought together with the high point of the Athenian imperial expansion during the middle/second half of the fifth century. Our earliest written evidence stems from exactly this period. Herodotus gives a rather brief version (8,55):

---

[16] It is, however, unclear which version of the myth or, rather, which moment of the contest is depicted (Hurwit 1999: 174).

[17] In a famous passage, Thucydides (1,2,5–6), too, reflects on the relationship between Attica's population and natural resources, claiming that Athens had never been conquered because the barrenness of its soil had never attracted outside aggressors.

In that acropolis is a shrine of Erechtheus, called the "Earthborn", and in the shrine are an olive tree and a pool of salt water. The story among the Athenians is that they were set there by Poseidon and Athena as tokens when they contended for the land. It happened that the olive tree was burnt by the barbarians with the rest of the sacred precinct, but on the day after its burning, when the Athenians ordered by the king to sacrifice went up to the sacred precinct, they saw a shoot of about a cubit's length sprung from the stump, and they reported this. (transl. A. D. Godley 1925)

While it is true that we do not have textual evidence that predates Herodotus, Marx has shown that the contest is attested in vase paintings from the sixth century, with images depicting Poseidon striking the ground with his trident and Athena with her spear (Marx 2011). Moreover, Herodotus' account makes clear that the highly symbolical aspect of the olive and its offshoot was already well known in the aftermath of Salamis – the astonishing number of variants also indicates that the story must have been part of the deep history of cultural memory. In a cultural ecological reading, the regenerative quality of the life-giving element is evocative of the regeneration of the community as a whole in the wake of destruction and debris. It might therefore be possible to interpret the evolution and symbolic quality of the story as interconnected with the historical experience of the Athenians in the fifth century. Storytelling, in other words, became a resource of its own, a narrative force vital to the restoration of civic identity and material regeneration in the face of catastrophe.

Storytelling and material environment were, in fact, brought together in a close-knit interdependency. As Hurwit puts it (1999: 229),

The visitor who traversed the summit of the Classical Acropolis was enmeshed in a network – an Acropolis-wide web – of meaning and reference. The web expanded organically as each new monument found itself in some fashion linked to monuments already there, unavoidably participating in a kind of discourse (both iconographic and stylistic) with other images or sites. The spectator who noted the reclining figure of Kekrops near the north angle of the Parthenon's west pediment, the marble (or bronze) olive tree of Athena at its center, had only to turn a little farther to the north to locate Kekrop's tomb, the "real" olive, and, probably, one or more images of Erechtheus again . . ..

Thus, the story of the gods' contest attaches special meaning to two significant topographical and cultic features on the Acropolis: the pool with salt water and the sacred olive remained important "storied" markers of place and mythic identity all throughout antiquity. The cult in the Erechtheion (about which we know frustratingly little) and its appearance on the west pediment of the Parthenon helped frame the mythical scene pictorially and practically in the Athenians' cultural imaginary. The important role of the imagination also comes to the fore when we consider the hydrological-geological features of the Acropolis: it is made up of limestone and there was certainly no natural pool of salt water on it. Thus, "If there was some kind of natural water on top of it, it must have been pure rain water, otherwise, the thalassa must have been an artificial basin, specifically constructed to underscore the credibility of the legend" (Patay-Horváth 2015: 355). While there is one objective description of the pool from antiquity as well as of the statues of the gods displaying their tokens (Pausanias 1,26,5), all archaeological traces have been lost due to architectural changes in later centuries.

Whether Poseidon had a cult on the Acropolis prior to the battle at Salamis is still unclear. By the end of the fifth century, however, Poseidon and Athena Polias shared the temple referred to (if only in two relatively late ancient sources) as the Erechtheion on the north side of the Acropolis. There was even an opening in the roof of its north porch and, throughout the centuries, Athenians pointed to marks in the rock below it where Poseidon's fabled trident was supposed to have struck (or, alternatively, where he or Zeus drove Erechtheus into the ground) (Elderkin 1941: 113).[18] It was another way of imbuing the natural landscape with a mythical narrative, explaining topographical features via highly imaginative images (Pausanias 1,26,5; Apollodorus 3,14,1). Athena Polias (i.e. "of the city"), on the other hand, attested to the chthonic roots of the goddess, the one worshipped by the Athenians' forefathers before her Olympian embodiments with the surnames Promachos and Parthenos became ever more prominent in the classical era (Papachatzis 1989: 176; Simon 1983: 68–69). All three variations of Athena had statues on the Acropolis, with the one in the Parthenon, wrought by Pheidias, as the most famous – it was 12 meters high and adorned in gold. In contrast, the statue of Athena Polias was made of olive wood and stood in her old temple, later in the Erechtheion. According to an old legend, it had fallen from heaven and was the holiest statue in Athens – an olive-oil lamp was supposedly burning in front of it day and night (Pausanias 1,26,6). And, every year, a team of maidens wove her a new dress (a *peplos*).[19]

---

[18] The figure of Erechtheus, according to legend the sixth king of Athens, is somewhat shrouded in mystery (Sourvinou-Inwood 2011: 51–88). One alternative name may have been Erichthonios, also known as an early king, or simply a variant (both mean "Very Earthly" or "Very Earthly Born", sprung from Ge Kourothropos). According to one version of the myth, Erichthonios was begotten by Hephaestos, who had chased after Athena, discharging his seed on the goddess' thigh, from where it fell to the earth and the snake god, Erichthonios, was born. Erechtheus was Athena's foster child (Homer *Iliad* 2,546–551), and his exact relation to Poseidon is unclear. In fact, Poseidon seems to have absorbed his identity by the mid-fifth century and the two were worshipped side by side (Hurwit 1999: 33). Poseidon-Erechtheus may have, in fact, shared some constitutive traits with Athena Polias, who was a vegetation and fertility goddess. His epithet Phutalmios means "producing or nourishing the plants" (Papachatzis 1989: 175–177).

[19] The complex ritual is described by Pausanias 1,27,2. Cf. Håland 2012: 258–262.

Myth and cult were important elements, constitutive of the civic identity and part of the religion of the *polis* community. But this observation hardly entails all layers of meaning. The story elements, the place names, and the gods' tokens were enmeshed in a social-ecological network of reference. In this context, I propose to interpret the tokens associated with Athena and Poseidon quite literally: as valuable resources vital to the life, identity, and (economic) survival of the community – and not just as "symbolic" abstractions (Patay-Horváth 2015: 356) or "merely" as "tokens of priority" where "the inherent value . . . was not the point" (Hurwit 1999: 32). In my understanding, the myth underscored an important ecological insight, namely that Athenian wealth and ecological well-being depended, to a large degree, on the olive and the fertility of the soil. The salt water may have "symbolized the navigation, sea trade, maritime power or some similar concept" (356), but it may also simply have stood for what it was: salt water, undrinkable and overall useless for the survival of the community.[20]

Water (de Cazanove 2015) certainly had its place in purification rituals and as a life-giving albeit destructive element, as attested to by Poseidon's wrath and the ensuing flood described earlier, but in Attica, which was overall characterized by a complex water ecology and chronic shortages, the olive and its agriculture had been even more central to the social-natural ecosystem in archaic and early classical times. This is also attested to in a later passage by Plutarch (*Themistocles* 19):

> After this he (Themistocles) equipped the Piraeus, because he had noticed the favorable shape of its harbors, and wished to attach the whole city to the sea; thus in a certain manner counteracting the policies of the ancient Athenian kings. For they, as it is said, in their efforts to draw the citizens away from the sea and accustom them to live not by navigation but by agriculture, disseminated the story about Athena, how when Poseidon was contending with her for possession of the country, she displayed the sacred olive-tree of the Acropolis to the judges, and so won the day. (transl. B. Perrin 1914)

Although this passage is far removed from the classical era, it still attests to the fact that there must have existed even older versions, and that those were explicitly situated in an agricultural venue (Patay-Horváth 2015: 358). We know that sacred ploughing took place on the north slope of the Acropolis. And there are various fertility cults attested with Athena Polias, with a strong agricultural connotation (Papachatzis 1989: 179).

This is particularly stressed by Håland (2012), who argues that "the importance of agriculture" is a central element in many of the various festivals "dedicated to the goddess of the olive crop" (256). Drawing on a range of sources and comparative anthropology, Håland has shown "that fertility is

---

[20] Cf. Elderkin (1941: 118–123) for an alternative interpretation.

crucial in the rituals and that women have an important role in carrying out the fertility cult" (257). This has to do with the fact that "the religious festivals of Athena follow a ritual calendar where celebrations were performed in connection with important phases during the ritual year of the olive" (258). The procession depicted on the Parthenon frieze, although certainly idealized, also showed participants carrying various offerings, including green branches that were probably offshoots from Athena's sacred olive trees (266).[21] And the victors in the greater Panathenaia received jars of olive oil (Aristotle *Politics* 6,4,1319b).

The Panathenic Games, according to one myth originally founded by were central to the civic identity in Athens and an important aspect of self-representation (Neils 2012). The victory of the Olympian deities over the Giants, which it commemorated (Sourvinou-Inwood 2011: 271–272), certainly had symbolic connotations that could point to the "annual victorious fight against the weather Gods" (Håland 2012: 269). These connotations were, however, part of an all-encompassing socio-cultural negotiation of the order of the natural ecosystem, on which agriculture and stockbreeding depended. "The popular calendar was a social representation of the order of nature, that is, of the 'natural' year" (271). Again, "renewal" and regenerative energies played an important role, most visible in the new *peplos* that Athena's statue received, replacing the old one (Sourvinou-Inwood 2011: 283).

If natural order was at stake, so was the social order: ritual was used to instantiate social hierarchies and status distinction. "The rules for participation in both Panathenaic games and the festival procession classified people into a complex hierarchy in which status was determined by age, gender, citizenship, wealth and social class" (Larson 2016: 148). It is, therefore, relatively easy to idealize words like "community" or "cohesion" in this context. The lived reality of Athens in classical times was one where different forms of violence were likewise present and where what we commonly refer to as religion was part of a framework built on imperial expansion and slave labor – in many ways, slavery is still one of the most underexamined realities of ancient environmental history and a paradigmatic example of what Nixon has termed "slow violence" (Nixon 2011). What I thus (maybe too emphatically) present as a storied ecology has to be taken with a grain of salt.

Then again, in many ways myth was characterized by the narrative negotiation of the experience of violence – in and between gods, communities, culture

---

[21] Twelve sacred olive trees stood, for instance, in the Academy, symbolizing the twelve *phratries* (brotherhoods) on Athens' territory. They were said to be descended from the very first olive tree. Cf. Herodotus 8,55; Pausanias 1,24,3.

and nature.[22] Myths could evoke powerful emotional and cognitive responses because the story world was founded upon reality and because it gave ample imaginative space to reflect on the social and spatial networks that connected the two:

> the story world of Greek myths is not a strongly secondary one, that is the secondary qualities that it does possess focus upon single events or single characters, and that those events or characters are often integrated into descriptions of the Primary World in such a way as to expand the possibilities of the latter, rather than to highlight the extraordinariness of the former. (Johnston 2018: 128)

The storied ecology of myth was a way of reflecting on present circumstances as much as it was a way of grounding present realities in the past; there was a reciprocity between these various chronological (and spatial) scales.

And, because present contexts affected future events, the continuity of mythical storytelling and ritual practice was constitutive of ancient societies' own survival – myths did not only "help to create and sustain beliefs" (Johnston 2018: 245); they were, I would argue, also central for passing on ecological knowledge (Eidinow 2016) and negotiating the intricate relationships that existed between human communities and the nonhuman, material environments where they settled. The myth of the contest between Athena and Poseidon is a good example in this context, because it highlighted the dependency of the community on the olive fruit and negotiated the spatial place-markers and ecological constraints (water supply) that were characteristic of the social-natural dynamic.

It is what could be termed a "sustainable story" because its rootedness in the deep history characteristic of Greek mythology brought together the "long-term perspective of culture-nature co-evolution and short-term concerns," while its "sensitivity to the multi-layered forms of relationality between . . . humans and the nonhuman world" reflected on aspects relevant "for the survival of the cultural ecosystem in its long-term co-evolution with natural ecosystems" (Zapf 2016b: 25).[23] Rather than solely presenting the close relationship between

---

[22] Animal sacrifice, for instance, was part of many rituals in the ancient world and intricately bound up – at least from our modern perspective – with aspects of systemic violence. To the ancients, the multi-sensorious experience of communal ritual was more important, however, and there was hardly any problematization of the very act of ritual animal slaughter in antiquity. Cf. Graf (2012); Osborne (2016).

[23] The locus classicus for discussing sustainability in antiquity is another story, presented by Plato *Kritias* 110e–111e, where Plato discusses the environmental decline when comparing the mythical landscape of Attica with what he perceives in the fourth century, including some insight into the interrelation between deforestation, soil erosion, and water management (Harris 2011; Hughes 2016: 22–26; Hughes 1994: 73–74; Thommen 2012: 40–41). While Plato's story is certainly important for various aspects of environmental history, my concern

polis and patron deity, the story helped render ecological insights into the social-natural system, its hydrological as well as biological features, passing them from generation to generation. It was, I would argue, part of the "ecology of mind" (Bateson 2000: 467–468), cognitively and emotionally staged in story and ritual practice, that connected the individual mind and body with a larger social-natural system of which the *polis* was only a part.

In order to trace the implications of this storied ecology in historical meaning and practice, I want to look at the place of the olive tree in ancient Athens, presenting what one might call an ecologized history.

A Rhizomatic Community: Landscape, Law, and an Ecologized History of the Olive

When we take up the dual project of a storied ecology and an ecologized history, it should be made clear that these two aspects cannot simply be disentangled from one another. They have to be seen as two sides of the same coin. In their insistent focus on history/stories and material relationships between humans and the environment, they also draw on a point made by Iovino and Oppermann, who argue that "the world's material phenomena are knots in a vast network of agencies, which can be 'read' and interpreted as forming narratives, stories. Developing in bodily forms and in discursive formulations, and arising in coevolutionary landscapes of natures and signs, the stories of matter are everywhere" (Iovino & Oppermann 2014: 1). We may borrow Iovino and Oppermann's concept of a "material ecocriticism" for an ecologized history in so far as this project also "examines matter both *in* texts and *as* a text, trying to shed light on the way bodily natures and discursive forces *express* their interaction whether in representations or in their concrete reality" (2; emphasis original). To read the mythic contest of Athena and Poseidon as a storied ecology, then, means to understand the narrative as expressing and negotiating the deep history of human settlement on the Athenian Acropolis and its embeddedness in a material, elemental environment – with concrete and complex feedback effects between human forms of cultural expression and natural forces.

The vast field of religious studies in the ancient world provides a good framework for reflecting on these entanglements. Regarding the human built environment and the natural environment in religious settings, Droogan writes: "a monument in the landscape, such as a temple, is at once a real solid material

---

here is more with the cultural ecology and its function for individual/communal minds when interacting with the material world. For a discussion of "sustainability" in antiquity from an interdisciplinary viewpoint, cf. Schliephake et al. (2020) (forthcoming).

thing, a social agent, a support for ideology and a contested site of varying sites of mythology" (Droogan 2013: 166). As we have seen, the Acropolis is a good example of a site where these different forms of agencies came together: it was constituted by the natural elements and landscape features, by the objects and buildings that surrounded them, and by stories that were told about the spatial and symbolical relationships between human community and the nonhuman environment.

Recent scholarship has focused on the way that religious practices and experiences were shaped by and emerged from the interplay of these cultural-material forces. "Such 'religion'," write Raja and Rüpke (2015: 4–5), "is understood as a spectrum of experiences, actions, and beliefs hinging on human communication with super-human or even transcendent agent(s)," where this communication "is not only using, but is shaped by, the very material and sensory basis of these activities." Interpreted as an embodied practice that takes the material frameworks as seriously as cultural narratives and social institutions, "religion" is then conceptualized as "the enlargement of the situationally relevant environment beyond the immediately plausible social environment of co-existing human beings (and frequently also animals)" (6). This is a decidedly posthuman take on ancient religion that is compatible with many approaches in the environmental humanities – some of which we'll trace in the last part of this Element.

One reason why these approaches can rub off onto each other is because ancient religion provides a glimpse, for us moderns, into how the ancients perceived the nonhuman world and its agency. But, although this outlook can be described as potentially posthuman, we nevertheless have to remind ourselves that it is context-dependent, dynamic, and framed from a human perspective above all. Some of our sources provide us with insights into how religious practices provided embodied experience and physical orientation in space, but this outlook can only be partial, dependent as it is on the respective source material and our interpretational tools. The phenomenon of landscape is such a heuristic instrument since the word connotes how cultures attribute meanings and value to their physical surroundings. "'Landscape' is about the symbolic perception of natural environment, about the way in which people read that environment for meaning" (McInerney & Sluiter 2016: 1). This is never a static affair but a highly "polyvalent" one (7), since these "meanings" are culturally and situationally activated – their dynamic, multivocal character is exactly where a historical analysis has to enter the debate in order to problematize and question approaches that may see an essentialist, or universal, quality in how humans have adapted and made meaning of their surroundings.

We have seen how "polyvalent" the myths associated with the Acropolis and the gods' contest remained over the centuries. This means that variations and transformations of the myth could be invoked and instrumentalized in different political contexts. Consequently, we have to take into consideration how human cultures have appropriated, transformed, and understood their physical environment not only in and through stories but also in and through architecture as well as shifting formations of political power. Thereby, it becomes possible to analyze not only how "terrain" has been "rendered into text" (15) over the course of history but also how texts have reflected on the interdependency of human meaning-making and the nonhuman world.

In an innovative reading, Margaret Miles (2016) has analyzed why Greek temples were built in the places where they were, and how they interacted with the surrounding landscape to create a specific ambience and to enable sensory experience that reinforced their "sacred" quality. In this context, the interplay between cultural as well as natural elements was crucial. As Miles puts it,

> The immediate green landscape around sanctuaries supported a sacred environment, and its care and regulation were supervised by personnel of the sanctuary or *polis*. A temenos often included both "cultivated" and "wild" elements of the landscape (groves, plants and birds) alongside man-made votives and buildings. Such an environment could recall or even evoke divine presence through the contrasting elements in the microcosm of the temenos, since the deities themselves partake of both cultivated and wild. (170)

Her observation fits in well with the environmental aspects stressed earlier and also helps in highlighting the particular quality of the sacred olive tree on the Acropolis.[24] It was indicative of "how elements of nature were featured in the sanctuary so as to evoke a numinous atmosphere, even supplying 'proofs' of past events" (175). The numinous quality certainly had to do with the fact that the tree was understood as consecrated to Athena, not only as her property but also as a historical testimony. Just as the tree was rooted in the soil, so, too, was the community; both were entangled and almost inseparable.

The Acropolis in general was densely populated with rustic shrines, gardens, and groves with rows of trees (some of which, as an inscription usually dated to 418 BCE indicates, even belonged to Athena herself and were seen as a loan from the goddess (Greco 2010: 132–136 and 421)). As Neudecker (2015: 226) interprets this particular setting, "These gardens acquired religious significance due to their constant need for upkeep, provided by the cult." Sacred landscape, then, entails both cultural narrative and the material practice of working the soil.

---

[24] On "sacred trees" in Roman religion cf. Hunt (2016). For a reflection of how (olive) trees and plants could be seen as an "expression of divine purpose" cf. Clark (1996).

This underlines, once again, the connection to fertility and the wider socio-economic context of agriculture. The fruits of the earth are a central component of autarchy, not deriving their value from the abstract value of economic circulation (Vernant 2016 [1996]: 295).[25]

However, this is only part of the picture of the olive's history in antiquity. As Horden and Purcell put it in *The Corrupting Sea*, the olive is certainly "among the most conspicuous symbols of Mediterranean landscape and life" (2000: 209). And this has to do with economic reasons above all:

> It offers numerous advantages in the economy of risk. The habitat of the tree is limited by temperature rather than precipitation .... It is tolerant of drought; but it is also a natural performer of exactly that acrobatic adjustability to which the canny human producer aspires, automatically responding to any benefit of extra moisture that may be available by cropping more generously without further help. (209)[26]

Moreover, it does not demand much attention and can be combined with other fruits in polycultural settings. The tree is thus a highly flexible agent in its own right, easily accommodating to "many agricultural and economic regimes" (Foxhall 2007: 1).

The olive is situated at the intersection between nature and culture. While the environmental conditions outlined earlier determine the natural-material framework that situates it within a specific Mediterranean ecology, its cultivation was a central element in ancient life. The olive has been vital to Mediterranean nutrition since antiquity, with cereals and vines making up the other parts of a "naturecultural" trinity. The olive and its oil continue to serve as staples of diet and major sources of fat in many Mediterranean countries. They are part of any history of the body (in terms of both food and skin care), of the ancient economy, and of the environment in antiquity – even of the history of night and day; after all, filling lamps for illumination was a central material practice in premodernity. As Foxhall muses, "The cultivation of the olive offers the opportunity to explore the intricate relationship between social and cultural

---

[25] This is, at least, the stance taken in (Ps.-)Aristotle *Economics* 1,1343b:

> Agriculture is the most honest of all such occupations; seeing that the wealth it brings is not derived from other men. Herein it is distinguished from trade and the wage-earning employments, which acquire wealth from others by their consent; and from war, which wrings it from them perforce. It is also a natural occupation; since by Nature's appointment all creatures receive sustenance from their mother, and mankind like the rest from their common mother the earth. (trans. G. C. Armstrong)

[26] It is probably for this reason that the sacred olive on the Acropolis grew in front of the Erechtheion in the Pandrosion, the open-air sanctuary of the Dew Goddess, Pandrosos, who was named after dew (Håland 2012: 272).

values, agricultural practices, the development and adoption of technology, and the workings of the economies of Greece – aspects of the ancient world which are sometimes studied in isolation from one another" (2007: 1).

Foxhall's monograph *Olive Cultivation in Ancient Greece: Seeking the Ancient Economy* (2007) offers a vivid portrait of these social-natural dynamics and, in general, the economic history of the olive from the Bronze Age to Late Antiquity has been well documented. These studies all contribute to an ecologized history of the ancient world, and it would take a meta-study to do justice to the impressive scope of their outlook; all the more so as this study would make clear that there is no such thing as one ecologized history of the olive; rather, there are many. As Foxhall argues, "The question of scale had a profound effect on the whole agronomic system, right down to the pruning of olive trees and the details of propagating young plants" (3). Moreover, "the olive's very adaptability makes it easy to neglect the effects of ecological differences on cultivation strategies and techniques" (3). The interplay, already outlined, between the narratives and practices that frame the social-material relationship between human culture and natural matter are crucial to any environmental approach to the ancient world. In fact, one of the reasons why the olive lends itself as a protagonist of environmental history is its biological parameters and growth cycles, which are largely outside anthropogenic control.

The olive, in combination with climate and soil, is a historical agent in its own right – although not necessarily in the sense that it can be seen as a transformative factor of socio-political processes (Foxhall 2007: 15). Rather, both aspects have to be seen as reciprocal and relational. There is evidence that allows a reconstruction of olive cycles, especially at Athens (Horden & Purcell 2000: 211–212), but the data is hard to validate, all the more so because the sources are often written from a perspective that does not say much about how growth cycles and yield impacted the population as a whole, or that deals with time periods for which our knowledge is rudimentary at best. For instance, a famous law attributed to the early Athenian lawgiver Solon (sixth century BCE) stated that all Athenian products were exempt from export – except oil (Plutarch *Solon* 24). This does not say as much about the availability of the resource in the Archaic Period as it says about the central role of the olive in the Athenians' cultural imaginary: as home to the first olive, Athens could present itself as the place that had established the olive's role in the Mediterranean. Aspects of the natural ecosystem were thus integrated into cultural self-representation.

Studying the history of the olive also means studying social hierarchy and access to resources. The olive tree was "fitted into a regime of property which is for social and political reasons ultra-fragmented" and which is, at the same time, part of the economy of "investment agriculture in the Mediterranean" (Horden & Purcell 2000: 210–211). Athens and Attica are cases in point, because we have well-documented source material that shows how the cultivation of the olive worked on large estates and became entwined with socio-technological developments that had to do with slave labor, on the one hand, and innovations, on the other. Oil presses and amphoras were central to extending the range of productions and oversea trade, making the olive an integral part of a lucrative, even speculative economy, regulated by the elite and the mechanisms of an aleatory redistribution system (212).

In Athens, this socioeconomic aspect continued to be framed in religious terms. As has already been mentioned, Athena's tree on the Acropolis was not only seen as belonging to the citizen community; it was even said to have founded this community in the first place (Detienne 1970). The other olive trees that could be found in Athens and Attica were said to have developed from its offshoots; firmly rooted in the soil, they made up what we may call a rhizomatic community that was part of the human settlement and at the same time stood apart from it. The image of the rhizomatic community is meant to underline the material processes that made up the ecological frameworks in which olives could grow, a network of entanglements and connections removed from human perception; moreover, it is meant to highlight the web of interrelated agencies between the natural growth cycle and cultural forms of symbolization. It is also an apt metaphor for an ecologized history, as it is not so much concerned with explaining these biophilic ties from a human actor–centered perspective; rather, it gives voice to the multiple, interrelated agencies that were constituting factors within a community of different lifeforms sharing a mutual environment.

In the ancient world, "sacred law" was one way of discursively articulating an understanding of the human interaction with transcended powers and natural forces that we could term rhizomatic or ecological. Like landscape, sacred law is a modern concept and has functioned as a heuristic instrument to deal with "inscriptional texts, which are often set up in sanctuaries they relate to, detailing and prescribing various aspects of organization and of worship in Greek cults, and hence to representing invaluable first-hand testimonies for the historical realities of Greek religious practices" (Petrovic 2015: 339). In many ways the term is misleading, because many of these texts were not formal laws but, rather, rules of behavior in certain cults or gave testimony to existing customs. A number of these texts, however, also openly address forms of behavior (within a sanctuary or a wider spatial context) with strong environmental or ecological underpinnings.

This is a point made by Cordovana and Chiai in their recently published collection of essays on *Pollution and the Environment in Ancient Life and*

Thought, where the contributions deal with a "selection of documentary sources" – many of which stem from sanctuaries or sacred precincts – that "considered together with the archaeological evidence, . . . show the presence of a common-sense environment" in antiquity, and especially "the shared sensibility for a clean environment" (2017: 12). In Chiai's essay in the same volume, for instance, it is convincingly shown how "sacralization allowed the local authorities to use religion and the power of the gods to the purpose of protecting the rivers and waters against environmental pollution" (2017: 79). One famous example of a sacred law stems from an inscription in Athens, usually dated to 430 BCE, which prohibited the washing of coats of sacrificed animals in the river near the sanctuary of Heracles (78). What was at stake in this description was certainly, on the one hand, the purity and integrity of the sacred precinct,[27] but, on the other hand, there is an understanding of environmental interconnectivity at work, which took the fluidity of the river seriously as an agent in its own right. The personified river could carry polluted water far outside the narrow district of the temple with negative repercussions for the entire (rhizomatic) community.

There were numerous sacred laws associated with the olives in and around Athens. Even if they stood on private property, the olive trees were deemed to belong to the goddess Athena; they could not be owned, nor were they secularized. According to a forensic speech of Lysias, there was a specific commission, overseen by the Areopagus (one of the oldest, albeit not one of the most important or powerful, state institutions), which controlled the stand of the olive trees on a regular basis (Lysias 7,25). This commission checked that the immediate surroundings of the olive trees were not built on or put to use in any other way.

The Areopagus seems to have – at least temporarily – met regularly to debate the overall state of the sacred olive trees; it notified the highest official (*archon*) of the number of trees and their location, which was important for the annual levy of oil, and it could sanction those who had violated the regulations concerning the trees, for instance by building in their vicinity or even by uprooting them (Horster 2006). This is also the context of Lysias' speech: it was written for a prosperous Athenian who, at the beginning of the fourth century BCE, had been charged with removing a sacred *sekos* (7,2). It is not entirely clear whether the term *sekos* refers to the stub of an olive tree (maybe of one of those trees harmed during the Peloponnesian War against Sparta and her allies) or a kind of small enclosure meant to protect it. Nonetheless, the speech

---

[27] On this subject see also Ekroth (2017). Purity and pollution have long been identified as central parts of any history of ancient Greek religion. A standard text is still Parker (1983); a more recent discussion and overview of the debate can be found in Carbon & Peels-Matthey (2018).

in general is a fascinating testament to how objects of the nonhuman world could enter the debate of a law court; in ancient Athens, trees were thus part of a decidedly sociopolitical setting. During late classical times, olive trees were still protected by law (Demosthenes 43,71) and they remained crucial to the Athenian self-image and the overall workings of society.[28]

To return to the question posed at the outset of this section: yes, olive trees did have standing in ancient Athens. They were bestowed with a special sacred aura and thereby implicitly protected for further generations. But this is only part of the bigger picture: of course, the economic benefit attached was an important factor, and the legal case of Lysias may have more to do with inner social conflicts and resentments in a postwar environment. Nonetheless, olive trees are a case in point for discussing the way nature and culture were not separate realms in the ancient world. In the myths, histories, and laws connected to the olive we are already confronted with, in Haraway's term (2003), a "natureculture," problematizing and breaking up binary worldviews and illustrating how the social and the natural are entwined in a complex dynamic that is both cultural and material. Ancient religion, I would argue, made up the in-between space of this encounter; it was the realm where the ancients thought about their own standing in the world and entered into a dialogue with forces different from themselves.

4. Coda: Ancient Thought and Contemporary Environmental Theory

What is the role of ancient myth in contemporary environmental theory?

Interestingly enough, inquiry into this question constitutes a blank and has not been dealt with systematically (Junquera & Moreno 2018: 1–2). This is all the more surprising as, on the one hand, there are many mythological figures, motifs, and structures in environmental discourse – from Gilgamesh and Eden all the way to Gaia and Prometheus – and, on the other, because classical reception studies have become a major paradigm of interdisciplinary debate. That this issue does not seem to have been taken up in any study may have to do with the ubiquity of the classical canon – we have become so used to many images and narratives borrowed from antiquity that we do not even bother to look into their respective historical contexts and their tradition.

We should. Because, as Holmes has recently argued, "the timeless value of classicism's objects (and texts) is so much given that these objects are always at risk of standing only as empty symbols of timelessness itself, silent rebukes to

---

[28] For laws protecting the environment in the ancient world cf. also Adam (1999) and Fargnoli (2012).

contestations over value" (Holmes 2017: 24). But value is what is increasingly at stake in a time of ecological crisis (Lane 2011), all the more so as debate over norms and ethics always involves transhistorical inquiry into how certain values and worldviews have been shaped and contested over time. Rather than view ancient myth and the epoch as a whole as something static and finished, we should follow Holmes' invitation to see it as something "liquid" and dynamic: "What is ancient can be awakened in the present as a younger contemporary rather than a distant ancestor" (Holmes 2017: 44).

In the following, I want to trace these different temporalities by analyzing their presence and role in contemporary environmental discourse. This is actually a subject that calls for a much more extensive and encompassing study, so my thoughts will remain only cursory. I aim to show how vital and important ancient culture still is today and how it can help in reflecting on our current predicaments with different and oftentimes surprising insights that can offer new perspectives in resituating humankind in a world teeming with countless nonhuman agents and companions.

Ancient Thought and/as Modern Environmental Theory

In the Tanner Lectures on Human Values of 1998, one of the preeminent scholars of ancient cultural history and religion, Walter Burkert, argued that "the crisis of science, the crisis of 'nature', and the crisis of tradition are interconnected." In his view, two central intellectual movements of the late twentieth century, postmodernity and social constructivism, had contributed to shaking up some of the core values and beliefs upon which the modern world had been built – on the one hand, trust in scientific facts had increasingly crumbled and, on the other hand, cultural tradition had lost its footing in an increasingly globalized, albeit multicultural, world of mass communication. Yet, Burkert was convinced of two things: first, that we need a "theoretical world independent from social differences and dynamics" and, second, that a dialogue with the ancient Greeks and their culture still constitutes an important framework for thinking within an abstract, imaginative space with powerful implications for the present. To him, the "decisive discovery of classical Greece" was the "construction of a 'theoretical world' which became the world of science .... The uniqueness of the Greek project," as he termed it, "is the faith in verifiable reality, a kosmos of physis."

Burkert did not understand this project as a return of sorts from *logos* to *mythos* but, rather, as an open debate that would, ideally, lead to what he called "consensual knowledge," a knowledge based on relationality, reciprocity, and intersubjectivity – both between humans and between humans and the world:

There remains the fact, even in a computer culture, that we cannot get rid of the "necessities of nature," as Antiphon said, to breathe, to eat, to hear and to see. We remain earth-dwellers on one globe from which we cannot escape. And whether we speak of the "universe" or of "nature," we are using Greek names and concepts. Of course names are not important; but reality makes itself felt. "Nature" as a basic concern, as a power not to be disregarded, has come back with the environmental movement. Still, the "environmental" perspective remains anthropocentric, nay egocentric: nature environs us but we remain at the center. The theoretical world picture should be more capacious and imaginative (Burkert 1999).

Although written twenty years ago, Burkert's words still strike a powerful chord today. The world has experienced not only one of the biggest revolutions in communication and cultural expressions with the advent of the internet and computer technology but also an ecological crisis unprecedented on a global scale. But the energy-intensive cultural revolution has not led to an uprooting of the anthropocentrism that Burkert saw at work toward the end of the millennium; quite the contrary. Electronic waste has entered the long list of anthropogenic ecological effects unknown before in the history of humankind.

Important as they are, Burkert's reflections nonetheless carry the danger of forwarding a romanticized notion of the ancient Greeks' outlook on the natural environment. Already in classical times we can find a strong anthropocentric stance in philosophy, one that was well aware that other, nonhuman powers shared the same *kosmos* but that still attributed to humankind a special place within it. In Sophocles' *Antigone*, arguably still the most performed ancient play, the chorus famously sings:

> Numberless wonders, terrible wonders walk the world
> but none the match for man . . .
> Man the master, ingenious past all measure,
> past all dreams, the skills within his grasp –
> he forges on, now to destruction,
> now again to greatness
> (Sophocles *Antigone* 332–366; transl. Fagles 1982).

It would be tempting to interpret these lines, which also include a description on how human technology is used to carry away the earth by plowing, to catch and kill animals, to domesticate the wild, and to build shelters from natural forces, as the first description of what we now term the Anthropocene. It is a meditation on achievement – and its inherent dangers, some of which might actually lead to self-destruction. But this would be taking a step too far. The setting is that of a *polis* community, and what is primarily at stake is not *physis* but *nomos* and *dike*, conceptions of order and justice on which the communal life depended.

Humankind and what being "human" means stand at the center of the tragedy, and, although humankind is depicted as being able to manage and master much of the nonhuman world, there are still powers eluding human influence or comprehension. If the lines are evocative of our own situation, then, because the Anthropocene confronts us again with an inquiry into our own capabilities and limits, this question, not our ecological crisis as such, is what had been prefigured by ancient Greek philosophy. As Raaflaub puts it, "The Greeks thus realized early on that man is ultimately responsible for his own and his community's well-being" and their "intellectual adventure" can best be analyzed and described as "placing man in the center of concentric circles that define his relation to household, community, the divine, and the larger outside world" (2016: 128). We have, in other words, always been *anthropos*. But that should not stand in the way of finding the new creative forms of renegotiating what our place is in nature.

In the theoretical debate, "nature," too, has come under increasing strain (Morton 2007) – mostly because the term has been crudely instrumentalized in the course of history (for racist ideologies as well as for the exploitation of resources, among other things). But then, again, the term has a long cultural tradition. Undoubtedly, *physis* was an important concept in Greek philosophy and treatises on medicine, the body, and the growth of plants.[29] However, already in antiquity what Burkert refers to as the "kosmos as physis" could mean different things at different times and in different cultures. It was a dynamic concept, and we should be wary of attributing uniformity to a vast body of sources and knowledge that was, in fact, more heterogeneous than we would like to admit. In its nuances and layers of meaning it is probably even closer than we are aware to some of our own theoretical notions. As Holmes puts it,

> However much we may want to throw out "nature" altogether or sideline it . . ., it still remains deeply embedded in how we organize our own thinking

---

[29] Recently, there has been some reflection on the Greek term *physis*. Based on Amerindian cosmologies, Descola (2005) has, for instance, argued that the Western dichotomy between "nature" and "culture" is only one of many possible ontologies. He also holds that the ancient Greeks did not use *physis* for a holistic concept of "nature" but, rather, for describing individual traits of specific plants or animals. The human and nonhuman world were thus, according to him, not seen as separate spheres but were perceived in their interactive potential. This is an interesting thought, but Descola's outlook is limited in so far as he mainly draws on archaic and classical sources. If we take the Hellenistic period into account, we would find a dynamic evolution of the concept of *physis*/"nature" that can be demonstrated in a plethora of texts. I would argue that this has to do not with technological advancement (although the Hellenistic age is full of innovation on many levels) but, rather, with political, cultural, social, and religious developments – but that would be the subject of another Element. Some preliminary thoughts can be found in Glacken (1967: 116–149).

about the non-human world, haunting forms of scientific inquiry and the epistemic modes of literature alike. It therefore still shapes what we look for when we turn to the past, and especially the Greco-Roman past, to challenge or enrich contemporary conceptual work. In negotiating with the ancient evidence, we can neither dismiss the category of nature as altogether misleading but nor is physis as familiar as it may seem. The relations of continuity and discontinuity that we construct in pursuing ecocriticism or Environmental Humanities in relationship to Greco-Roman antiquity thus carry their own dangers but also their own promise. Neither radically other nor overly familiar, the ancient material, together with its complex reception history, holds the potential to animate in its own way what we might call an untimely ecology at a moment when ecological thinking has become especially fertile ground. (Holmes 2017: xii)

Holmes' notion of an "untimely ecology" is an apt way of thinking about the interconnection between antiquity and the present moment. Every act of reception appropriates and interprets antiquity anew, and potentially as never before; but, nonetheless, this act of reception stands in a line of tradition. It has to find its own identity and place in the theoretical or cultural landscape by actively entering into a dialogue with different times and voices. And, through this encounter, new knowledge and new imaginative capacity to envision alternative "world pictures" in Burkert's sense can be sought.

The transformative and transcultural potential of ancient culture is crucial in this respect. When we employ classical texts for ecological thinking in the present, it is important neither to integrate antiquity all too swiftly into contemporary worldviews nor to read the evidence anachronistically by bringing present predicaments and convictions to bear on material that stems from a completely different background. The same holds true for how we deal with nature and culture. If we want to think human history and geostory together, it is vital "to take both their difference and their interrelatedness into account as necessary conditions of their theoretical and textual explorations" (Zapf 2016a: 4). As Zapf puts it, "connectivity *and* difference are the two basic axioms of an ecological epistemology" (4, emphasis in original).

In his reinterpretation of pre-Socratic philosophy, David Macauley, for instance, writes: "By returning critically to ecological origins in Presocratic thought, we may observe some of the historical 'roots' of Western perceptions of the natural world and, given time and patience, perhaps eventually witness the flowering of this ancient wisdom in contemporary environmental actions" (Macauley 2010: 136).[30] His reflections (just like my own regarding the role of

---

[30] J. Baird-Callicott has recently drawn a similar connection to pre-Socratic natural philosophy in his insistent call for a new moral philosophy (one that he refers to as "NeoPresocratic") that bridges the divide between the humanities and the sciences, holding that "facts are theory-laden

olive trees in ancient Athens developed earlier) echo the "rhizomatic philoso-phy" (136) of Gilles Deleuze and Félix Guattari in *A Thousand Plateaus* (2004 [1980]). This de-hierarchized organization of knowledge and world description, which is open to change and develops analogies between different areas of philosophical and scientific inquiry that seemingly do not have much in com-mon, could prove vital for the environmental humanities. This is because it entails the potential of creating montages of knowledge across vast spans of time and space, thus bringing about new forms of nonstandardized knowledge with new relations and interdependencies. It forces us, in other words, to move beyond the narrow boundaries of the Anthropocene in order to make room for premodern thoughts and worldviews – as both challenge and chance.

One ancient mythological figure that has figured prominently in the environ-mental debate is the primordial Greek earth-goddess Gaia. When the atmo-spheric geochemist James Lovelock formulated the idea that our planet functions similarly to an animate organism by emphasizing the elemental role of the air and the atmosphere in supporting the development and protection of the biosphere, he used the figure of Gaia to personify this self-regulating principle of life (1979). Despite criticism (Schneider & Boston 1991), Lovelock's "Gaia hypothesis" has stuck. Put simply, it proposes that the Earth is able to support itself in a manner similar to a complex living system with the help of cybernetic and material processes that regulate the composition of the atmosphere, the oceans, and the soil, whereby organic life plays an important role in the ceaseless modulation of the planet's climate. Gaia, in Lovelock's terms, helps render the earthly world as a living entity. As the eco-philosopher David Abram comments on the theory,

> Whatever the scientific fate of the Gaia hypothesis, its emergence provides a striking illustration of the way in which a renewed awareness of the air forces us to recognize, ever more vividly, our interdependence with the countless organisms that surround us, and ultimately encourages us to speak of the encompassing earth in the manner of our oral ancestors, as an animate, living presence. (Abram 1996: 302n62)

It is unclear whether Abram's emphatic reception also has in mind the ancient Greeks and their oral poetry, but they have certainly made an appearance in Bruno Latour's latest monograph, *Facing Gaia* (2017), developed out of his Gifford Lectures at Edinburgh in 2013. Harking back to Hesiod, Latour first explains that Gaia is a "force from the time before the gods," "a terrifying power ... dark-skinned, dark-haired, and somber" (81–83). This leads him, in

---

and theories are value-laden" (Callicott 2017: 136 and 153). Some of his arguments have been prefigured by Tress (2002). A different approach to ancient philosophy is found in Sallis (2016).

a next step, to engage in an erudite rereading of Lovelock's initial theory to explain that Lovelock's Gaia should not be mistaken as a deified, holistic entity, as many modern recipients have done. Rather, in Latour's interpretation, Gaia is an innovative take on the problem of "understand(ing) in what respect the Earth is active, but *without endowing it with a soul*" and "in what respect can one say that it *retroacts to the collective actions of humans*" (86; emphasis in original). Latour's Gaia, distilled from Lovelock's, is born from "the paradox . . . that the name of a proteiform, monstrous, shameless, primitive goddess has been given to what is probably the *least religious entity* produced by Western science" (87; emphasis in original). As Latour convincingly argues, "Gaia is not an organism" and "we cannot apply to it any technological or religious model. It may have an order, but it has no hierarchy" (106); it "is a creature no more of chance than of necessity. Which means that it closely resembles what we have come to regard *as history itself*" (107; emphasis in original).

The reception of the ancient mythological figure Gaia is therefore probably not the best case for arguing that ancient thought plays (or should play) a role in contemporary environmental theory. Obviously, the reception process always entails a danger of misreading or misinterpretation. Moreover, it is doubtful whether Lovelock's Gaia even counts as a conscious act of reception, since the ancients hardly come to the fore in his theory. He used an ancient vessel but without the ingredients – a fact that Latour recognizes and rectifies, but not entirely. As Latour summed up his lecture series:

> Gaia . . . is the Earth understood not as system but as what has a history, what mobilizes everything in the same geostory. Gaia is not Nature, nor is it a deity. In order to face a secular Gaia, we need to extract ourselves from the amalgam of Religion and Nature. It is a new form of political power that has to be explored through a renewed attempt at political theology composed of those three concepts: demos, theos and nomos. It is only once the multiplicity of people in conflicts for the new geopolitics of the Anthropocene is recognized, that the "planetary boundaries" might be recognized as political delineations and the question of peace addressed. (Latour 2013)

Latour's terminology is evocative of Greek philosophy and political theory, but the historical differences are as central as the act of reception. Gaia is neither a goddess nor a mythological archetype but, rather, a new category dissolving the boundaries between human and nonhuman agency in the Anthropocene, with new forms of political representation and participation (a new "political theology").

When we turn to one of the first texts of the Greek Archaic, namely Hesiod's *Theogony*, then it becomes quite clear where the differences between Hesiod's and Latour's Gaia lie (although Latour, interestingly enough, replicates some of

Hesiod's highly misogynist terminology in the preceding quotes). In Hesiod's *Theogony*, which depicts the genesis of the gods and the world, offering a fully developed cosmogony, Gaia is both the firm terrestrial body, the habitat of all life, and the anthropomorphized primordial goddess central to the emergence of the first generation of the gods as well as of the sky, the mountains, and the sea. Gaia is both person as well as abstraction, a way to reflect on genealogy and the force of natural matter. She cannot be equated with a naturalistic explanation of natural phenomena but, rather, must be seen as part of a network where human transgression entails punishment by the gods.

As Raaflaub notes, "Hesiod uses genealogical connections – and thus abstraction – to systematize the manifold forces that influence human society and well-being" and the account as a whole is highly politicized, eventually presenting "Zeus' new order as exemplary of leadership based on justice and fairness" (Raaflaub 2016: 131). Genealogy is, indeed, the "backbone" (West 1966: 31) of Hesiod's text. It is part of what we could describe (using one of Latour's terms) as a "metaphoric zone" (Latour 2017: 86), the sphere that brings forth, through manifold poietic metamorphosis, the gods, heroes, and material phenomena as acting agents. It is a highly imaginative and creative act, one that finds its newest (cultural-)genealogical expression in our own times.

But, if the constraints and risks attached to the enterprise of including ancient myth or philosophy into contemporary environmental theory are so high, why should we bother at all with this material? For one thing, the Gaia debate shows that is worthwhile to look into the ancient contexts and meanings because otherwise we are running the risk of creating a mytho-poetical theory ourselves, one that is uncritical of intellectual origins and more concerned with an "invention of tradition" (Hobsbawm & Ranger 1983) than historical critique. On the other hand, our cultural inventory and theoretical tools are so tightly interwoven with antiquity that we cannot help but critically resituate our own situation and debate with regard to this past. This also means to take seriously not only the connections but also the differences operating across multiple scale levels, temporal and spatial, between present and past. It is probably, as Adamson has suggested, most productive to think of ancient mythological presences like Gaia as "seeing instruments" (2016: 136) that help in imaginatively discerning how to live in a world characterized by various agencies and interdependencies, social and biophilic.[31] Developing new "seeing instruments" with the help of premodern ecological knowledge and insight is one of the central tasks that the

---

[31] Adamson has also drawn on "multispecies ethnography" and the "cosmovision" of Amerindian cosmologies in this context (Adamson 2014 and 2017), and it would be a worthwhile task to discern the connections made in contemporary ethnographic literature between ancient culture and indigenous worldviews in greater depth.

classics and ancient history can contribute to the interdisciplinary project of the environmental humanities.

Summary

This Element has been concerned with illustrating the connections between Greco-Roman antiquity and our modern environmental crisis. As I have tried to show, there are some limits to this exchange, which have to do with misinterpretation as well as with materiality – many of the environmental perils and toxic substances that modernity has created were wholly unknown in the ancient world. Ecologically and geologically speaking, the current debate surrounding the term "Anthropocene" very much deals with a decidedly modern phenomenon – if we take into account, for instance, that the beach shores of the volcanically active islands of Hawaii have in recent years become littered with what have been termed "plastiglomerates" (new types of rock cobbled together from plastic, volcanic rock, sediments, and corals), then it becomes ultimately clear that we are now, indeed, witnessing a new era in the geohistory of the planet, one that is materially different from premodernity.

As I have argued in the course of this Element, there are two sides to the rise-and-fall narrative of the Anthropocene, however. The term ultimately invites associations that extend beyond the narrow confines of the modern era and that stretch all the way back to the first written (and visual) documents from antiquity (and the prehistoric period of our species). Already in the archaic period, Homer's and Hesiod's epic poetry (influenced by Near Eastern precursors) grapples with the question of what humankind's place is in the world. We only need to think of the famous description of Achilles' shield in the *Iliad* (18,478–608) to be confronted with an entire microcosm, depicting different ways of human life and social experience, but also embedded and encircled by a macrocosm of natural forces that interact with and frame the natural-cultural ecology.

Ecological frameworks and sociohistorical settings have drastically changed since the creation of the first written documents on which our entire text-based canon rests. But, if these texts still speak to us, then it becomes clear that they nonetheless contain an aesthetic quality and a cultural knowledge that is worth preserving and that has, time and again, helped to imaginatively reflect on the interaction between humans and their surroundings as well as the interconnections between times and places. We still need stories, maybe even myths, to orient ourselves in an increasingly fast-paced and confusing present. It is one of the quandaries of our times that we are witnessing the biggest cultural revolution in communication technology since the invention of the alphabet in antiquity just as climate change is happening. Unfortunately, this can divert attention and even lead to misinformation and to the undoing of scientific fact. This is why shared meaning and potentially transcultural narratives are ever more important as fundamental pillars in a time when climate change needs to be accompanied by culture change. To be sure, Homer and Hesiod do not contain any advice on how to deal with socio-technological disaster, but they attest to cultural sustainability, even resilience, and in their alterity they constitute a resource that tests and sharpens our understanding of historical context, the experience of otherness, and the workings of the (environmental) imagination.

But the reception of the ancient world in our present is not a one-way street. It is multidirectional and relational in that the experience of climate change and the emergence of new environmental theories as well as scientific paradigms affect our understanding of antiquity. As I have tried to show, there are now approaches to the ancient world that can be read as direct commentary on our own historical situation. What unites these approaches is that they make use of an ecological outlook, which takes the nonhuman world seriously as an agent in its own right, and, in turn, create new epistemological models for reflecting on how ancient societies organized themselves and dealt with environmental perils or contingency. The resulting ecologized history can be read as an attempt to think natural history and human political history together in their interdependencies and interactions.

Culturally speaking, the ancients made sense of their surrounding ecosystems and their relation to other forces (organic and supernatural) with the help of stories, practices, and highly symbolic acts of meaning-making. Theirs was a storied ecology that was vital to orientation in space, for the cultural creation of landscape and place attachment as well as for the development of social institutions, entailing hierarchies and systemic violence as well as including conceptions of justice and law. It should be stressed again that this argument does not say that an ecology in the sense of our modern science existed in antiquity (although there may have been some precursors). But it is a way of reflecting on how a sensitivity to natural processes as well as the manifold interconnections between human systems and their natural surroundings developed, and how it was eventually articulated in and through (mythological) stories as well as philosophical reasoning – a knowledge that certainly entailed insight into what we would call ecological processes and even an understanding of the need for protective measures both of the environment and of human settlements against natural forces.

I have tried to illustrate this dialectic of an ecologized history and a storied ecology with the help of ancient Athens and the vast area of religion in the classical period. The two cultural landmarks and resonant images of the ancient world – the Acropolis and the olive tree – interact in constituting a "natureculture" that still entails important insights into premodern storied ecologies with their manifold mythological, spatial, temporal, social, and cultural dimensions. If it is not underway already, then the time is ripe for an "ecological turn" in classical studies/ancient history (all the more so as scientific data sets – problematic as they still are – continue to expand our knowledge on, for instance, the ancient climate). Many of the motifs and symbols of the classical canon are very useful in this context because they are generally well known and carry their own weight as cultural sediments in a layered natural-cultural history. Or, to use another metaphor that would have made more sense to someone living in the ancient world, they are but small parts in the vast, vibrant mosaic we now refer to as the environmental humanities.

Bibliography

Abram, D. (1996). *The Spell of the Sensuous: Perception and Language in a More-Than-Human World.* New York: Vintage.

Adam, S. (1999). Environnement et droit dans l'Antiquité Grecque. In G. Thür and F. J. F. Nieto, eds., *Symposion 1999. Vorträge zur griechischen und hellenistischen Rechtsgeschichte.* Köln: Böhlau 2003, pp. 371–386.

Adams, S. (2003). Environnement et droit dans l'Antiquité Grecque. In G. Thür and F. Nieto, eds., *Symposion 1999: Vorträge zur griechischen und hellenistischen Rechtsgeschichte.* Köln: Böhlau, pp. 371–386.

Adamson, J. (2014). Source of Life: *Avatar, Amazonia,* and an Ecology of Selves. In S. Iovino and S. Oppermann, eds., *Material Ecocriticism.* Bloomington: Indiana University Press, pp. 253–268.

Adamson, J. (2016). Humanities. In J. Adamson, W. A. Gleason and D. Pellow, eds., *Keywords for Environmental Studies.* New York: New York University Press, pp. 135–139.

Adamson, J. (2017). We Have Never Been Anthropos: From Environmental Justice to Cosmopolitics. In S. Oppermann and S. Iovino, eds., *Environmental Humanities: Voices from the Anthropocene.* Lanham, MD: Rowman & Littlefield, pp. 155–174.

Alaimo, S. (2012). Sustainable This, Sustainable That: New Materialisms, Posthumanism, and Unknown Futures. *PMLA,* 127(3), 558–564.

Anderson, G. C. (1935). *Aristotle in 23 Volumes, Vol. 18.* Cambridge, MA: Harvard University Press.

Bateson, G. (1991). *A Sacred Unity: Further Steps to an Ecology of Mind.* New York: Harper Collins.

Bateson, G. (2000 [1972]). *Steps to an Ecology of Mind.* Chicago: University of Chicago Press.

Bateson, G. (2002). *Mind and Nature: A Necessary Unity.* Creskill: Hampton Press.

Bawden, G. & Reycraft, R. M., eds. (2000). *Environmental Disaster and the Archaeology of Human Response.* Albuquerque: University of New Mexico Press.

Berman, D. W. (2017). Cities-before-Cities. "Prefoundational" Myth and the Construction of Greek Civic Space. In G. Hawes, ed., *Myths on the Map: The Storied Landscapes of Ancient Greece.* Oxford: Oxford University Press, pp. 32–51.

Bresson, A. (2014). The Ancient World. A Climatic Exchange. In F. de Callataÿ, ed., *Quantifying the Greco-Roman Economy and Beyond.* Bari: Edipuglia, pp. 43–62.

Burkert, W. (1999). On "Nature" and "Theory": A Discourse with the Ancient Greeks. *Michigan Quarterly Review*, 38(2), hdl.handle.net/2027/spo. act2080.0038.205.

Callicott, J. B. (2017). Worldview Remediation in the First Century of the New Millennnium. In S. Oppermann and S. Iovino, eds., *Environmental Humanities: Voices from the Anthropocene*. Lanham, MD: Rowman & Littlefield, pp. 133–154.

Carbon, J.-M. & Peels-Mathey, S., eds. (2018). *Purity and Purification in the Ancient Greek World*. Liège: Presse Universitaire de Liège.

Castriota, D. (1992). *Myth, Ethos, and Actuality: Official Art in Fifth-Century B. C. Athens*. Madison: University of Wisconsion Press.

Chakrabarty, D. (2009). The Climate of History: Four Theses. *Critical Inquiry*, 35(2),197–222.

Chakrabarty, D. (2012). Postcolonial Studies and the Challenge of Climate Change. *New Literary History*, 43, 1–18.

Chiai, G. F. (2017). Rivers and Waters Protection in the Ancient World: How Religion Can Protect the Environment. In O. D. Cordovana and G. F. Chiai, eds., *Pollution and the Environment in Ancient Life and Thought*. Stuttgart: Franz Steiner Verlag, pp. 61–82.

Christian, D. (2005). *Maps of Time: An Introduction to Big History*. Berkeley: University of California Press.

Clark, G. (1996). Cosmic Sympathies: Nature as the Expression of Divine Purpose. In G. Shipley and J. Salmon, eds., *Human Landscapes in Classical Antiquity: Environment and Culture*. London: Routledge, pp. 310–330.

Clark, T. (2015). *Ecocriticism on the Edge: The Anthropocene as a Threshold Concept*. New York: Bloomsbury.

Clements, J. H. (2015). The Terrain of Autochthony: Shaping the Athenian Landscape in the Late Fifth Century BCE. In R. F. Kennedy and M. Jones-Lewis, eds., *The Routledge Handbook of Identity and the Environment in the Classical and Medieval Worlds*. London: Routledge, pp. 315–340.

Cohen, Jeffrey J., ed. (2012). *Animal, Vegetable, Mineral: Ethics and Objects*. Washington, DC: Oliphaunt Books.

Collard, C. & Cropp, M. (2008). *Euripides VII: Fragments. Aegeus-Meleager*. Cambridge, MA: Harvard University Press.

Cordovana, O. D. & Chiai, G. F. (2017). Introduction. The Griffin and the Hunting. In O. D. Cordovana and G. F. Chiai, eds., *Pollution and the Environment in Ancient Life and Thought*. Stuttgart: Franz Steiner Verlag, pp. 11–24.

Crutzen, P. J. & Stoermer, E. (2000). The "Anthropocene". *Global Change Newsletter*, 41, 17–18.

Dalby, S. (2016). Framing the Anthropocene: The Good, the Bad, and the Ugly. *The Anthropocene Review*, 3(1), 33–51.

Dalley, S. (2017). The Natural World in Ancient Mesopotamian Literature. In J. Parham and L. Westling, eds., *A Global History of Literature and the Environment*. Cambridge: Cambridge University Press, pp. 21–36.

de Cazanove, O. (2015). Water. In R. Raja and J. Rüpke, eds., *A Companion to the Archaeology of Religion in the Ancient World*. Malden, MA: Wiley Blackwell, pp. 181–193.

Deleuze, G. & Guattari, F. (2004 [1980]). *A Thousand Plateaus: Capitalism and Schizophrenia*. New York: Continuum.

Descola, Ph. (2005). *Par-delà nature et culture*. Paris: Gallimard.

Detienne, M. (1970). L'Olivier: un mythe politico-religieux. In M. I. Finley, ed., *Problèmes de la terre en Grèce ancienne*. Paris: Mouton, pp. 293–306.

Dods, M., Smith, J. J. & Wilson, G. (1948). *Augustine: De Civitate Dei*. New York: Hapfner.

Droogan, J. (2013). *Religion, Material Culture and Archaeology*. London: Bloomsbury.

Egerton, F. N. (2012). *Roots of Ecology: From Antiquity to Haeckel*. Berkeley: University of California Press.

Eidinow, E. (2016). Telling Stories: Exploring the Relationship between Myths and Ecological Wisdom. *Landscape and Urban Planning*, 155, 47–52.

Ekroth, G. (2017). "Don't Throw Any Bones in the Sanctuary!" On the Handling of Sacred Waste in Ancient Greek Cult Places. In C. Moser and J. Knust, eds., *Ritual Matters: Material Remains and Ancient Religion*. Ann Arbor: University of Michigan Press, pp. 33–51.

Elderkin, G. W. (1941). The Cults of the Erechtheion. *Hesperia*, 10, 113–124.

Emmett, R. S. & Nye, D. E. (2017). *The Environmental Humanities: A Critical Introduction*. Cambridge, MA: The MIT Press.

Erikson, K. (1991). A New Species of Trouble. In W. Endlicher et al., eds., *Communities at Risk: Collective Responses to Technological Hazards*. Berlin: Springer, pp. 1–13.

Fagles, R. (1982). *Sophocles: The Three Theban Plays*. New York: Viking Press.

Fargnoli, I. (2012). Umweltschutz und Römisches Recht? In I. Fargnoli and S. Rebenich, eds., *Das Vermächtnis der Römer: Römisches Recht und Europa*. Bern: Haupt Verlag, pp. 151–175.

Finke, P. (2006). Die Evolutionäre Kulturökologie: Hintergründe, Prinzipien und Perspektiven einer neuen Theorie der Kultur. *Anglia*, 124(1), 175–217.

Foxhall, L. (2007). *Olive Cultivation in Ancient Greece: Seeking the Ancient Economy*. Oxford: Oxford University Press.

Foxhall, L., Jones, M. & Forbes, H. (2007). Human Ecology and the Classical Landscape: Greek and Roman Worlds. In S. E. Alcock and R. Osborne, eds., *Classical Archaeology*. Malden, MA: Blackwell, pp. 91–117.

Frazer, J. G. (2016 [1921]). *The Library of "Apollodorus."* Hastings: Delphi Classics.

Garrard, G. (2014). Introduction. In G. Garrard, ed., *The Oxford Handbook of Ecocriticism*. Oxford: Oxford University Press, pp. 1–8.

Gehrke, H.-J. (1994). Mythos, Geschichte, Politik – antik und modern. *Saeculum*, 45(2), 239–264.

Ghosh, A. (2016). *The Great Derangement: Climate Change and the Unthinkable*. Chicago: The University of Chicago Press.

Glacken, C. J. (1967). *Traces on the Rhodian Shore: Nature and Culture in Western Thought from Ancient Times to the End of the Eighteenth Century*. Berkeley: University of California Press.

Godley, A. D. (1925). *Herodotus: The Persian Wars, vol. 4: Books 7 and 8*. Cambridge, MA: Harvard University Press.

Graf, F. (2012). One Generation after Burkert and Girard. Where Are the Great Theories? In C. A. Faraone and F. S. Naiden, eds., *Greek and Roman Animal Sacrifice: Ancient Victims, Modern Observers*. Cambridge: Cambridge University Press, pp. 32–51.

Greco, E. (2010). *Topografi di Atene: Sviluppo urbano e monumenti dale origini al III secolo d. C. Vol. I*. Athens: Scuola Archeologica Italiana di Atene.

Haber, W. (2007). Energy, Food, and Land – the Ecological Traps of Humankind. *Environmental Science & Pollution Research*, 14, 359–365.

Haber, W. (2016). Anthropozän – Folgen für das Verhältnis von Humanität und Ökologie. In W. Haber, M. Held and M. Vogt, eds., *Die Welt im Anthropozän. Erkundungen im Spannungsfeld zwischen Ökologie und Humanität*. München: oekom, pp. 19–38.

Håland, E. J. (2012). The Ritual Year of Athena: The Agricultural Cycle of the Olive, Girls' Rites of Passage, and Official Ideology. *Journal of Religious History*, 36(2), 256–284.

Haraway, D. (2003). *The Companion Species Manifesto: Dogs, People, and Significant Otherness*. Chicago: Chicago University Press.

Harper, K. (2017). *The Fate of Rome: Climate, Disease, and the End of an Empire*. Princeton, NJ: Princeton University Press.

Harris, W. V. (2011). Plato and the Deforestation of Attica. *Athenaeum*, 99, 479–482.

Harris, W. V., ed. (2013). *The Ancient Mediterranean between Science and History*. Leiden: Brill.

Hassan, F. A. (2004). Ecology in Archaeology: From Cognition to Action. In J. Bintliff, ed., *A Companion to Archaeology*. Malden, MA: Blackwell, pp. 311–333.

Hawes, G. (2017). Of Myths and Maps. In G. Hawes, ed., *Myths on the Map: The Storied Landscapes of Ancient Greece*. Oxford: Oxford University Press, pp. 1–13.

Heise, U. (2006). The Hitchhiker's Guide to Ecocriticism. *PMLA*, 121(2), 503–516.

Heise, U. (2017). Introduction: Planet, Species, Justice – and the Stories We Tell about Them. In U. Heise, J. Christensen and M. Niemann, eds., *The Routledge Companion to the Environmental Humanities*. London: Routledge, pp. 1–10.

Herrmann, B. (2013). *Umweltgeschichte. Eine Einführung in die Grundbegriffe*. Heidelberg: Springer.

Hobsbawm, E. & Ranger, T., eds. (1983). *The Invention of Tradition*. Cambridge: Cambridge University Press.

Holmes, B. (2014). Greco-Roman Ethics and the Naturalistic Fantasy. *Isis*, 105 (3), 569–578.

Holmes, B. (2015). Situating Scamander: "Natureculture" in the *Iliad. Ramus*, 44(1/2), 29–51.

Holmes, B. (2017). Foreword: Before Nature? In Ch. Schliephake, ed., *Ecocriticism, Ecology, and the Cultures of Antiquity*. Lanham, MD: Lexington Books, pp.ix–xiii.

Holmes, B. (2017). Liquid Antiquity. In B. Holmes and K. Marta, eds., *Liquid Antiquity*. Geneva: Deste, pp. 19–59.

Horden, P. & Purcell, N. (2000). *The Corrupting Sea: A Study of Mediterranean History*. Malden, MA: Blackwell.

Horster, M. (2006). Die Olivenbäume der Athena und die Todesstrafe. In H.-U. Rupprecht, ed., *Symposion 2003: Vorträge zur griechischen und hellenistischen Rechtsgeschichte*. Wien: Verlag der Österreichischen Akademie der Wissenschaften, pp. 167–185.

Hughes, J. D. (1994). *Pan's Travail: Environmental Problems of the Ancient Greeks and Romans*. Baltimore: John Hopkins University Press.

Hughes, J. D. (2014). *Environmental Problems of the Greeks and Romans*. Baltimore: John Hopkins University Press.

Hughes, J. D. (2016). *What Is Environmental History?* Cambridge: Polity Press.

Hunt, A. (2016). *Reviving Roman Religion: Sacred Trees in the Roman World*. Cambridge: Cambridge University Press.

Hurwit, J. M. (1999). *The Athenian Acropolis: History, Mythology, and Archaeology from the Neolithic Era to the Present.* Cambridge: Cambridge University Press.

Iovino, S. & Oppermann, S. (2014). Introduction: Stories Come to Matter. In S. Iovino and S. Oppermann, eds., *Material Ecocriticism.* Bloomington: Indiana University Press, pp. 1–17.

Irby, G. L., McCall, R. & Radini, A. (2016). "Ecology" in the Ancient Mediterranean. In G. L. Irby, ed., *A Companion to Science, Technology, and Medicine in Ancient Greece and Rome, Vol. I.* Chichester: Wiley Blackwell, pp. 296–312.

Irby-Massie, G. L. (2008). *Prometheus Bound* and Contemporary Trends in Greek Natural Philosophy. *Greek, Roman, and Byzantine Studies*, 48, 133–157.

Jenkins, A. (2007). Alexander von Humboldt's *Kosmos* and the Beginnings of Ecocriticism. *ISLE*, 14(2), 89–105.

Johnston, S. I. (2018). *The Story of Myth.* Cambridge, MA: Harvard University Press.

Junquera, I. M. & Moreno, F. M. (2018). Mythology and Ecocriticism: A Natural Encounter. Introduction. *Ecozon@*, 9(2), 1–7.

Kalof, L., ed. (2007). *A Cultural History of Animals. Vol. 1: Antiquity to the Dark Ages (2500 BC–1000 AD).* London: Bloomsbury.

Kennedy, R. F. & Jones-Lewis, M., eds. (2015). *The Routledge Handbook of Identity and the Environment in the Classical and Medieval Worlds.* London: Routledge.

Kerridge, R. (2017). Foreword. In S. Oppermann and S. Iovino, eds., *Environmental Humanities: Voices from the Anthropocene.* Lanham, MD: Rowman & Littlefield, pp. viii–xvii.

Kindt, J. (2012). *Rethinking Greek Religion.* Cambridge: Cambridge University Press.

Lane, M. (2011). *Eco-Republic: Ancient Thinking for a Green Age.* Oxford: Peter Lang.

Langin, K. (2018). Rise and Fall of Roman Empire Exposed in Greenland Ice Samples. *Science*, 14 May, doi:10.1126/science.aau1738.

Larson, J. (2016). *Understanding Greek Religion.* London: Routledge.

Latour, B. (2013). First of the Gifford Lectures given by Bruno Latour in Edinburgh February 2013, "Facing Gaia". www.bruno-latour.fr/node/487.

Latour, B. (2017). *Facing Gaia: Eight Lectures on the New Climatic Regime.* Cambridge: Polity.

LeMenager, S. (2017). The Humanities after the Anthropocene. In U. Heise, J. Christensen and M. Niemann, eds., *The Routledge Companion to the Environmental Humanities*. London: Routledge, pp. 473–481.

Lovelock, J. (1979). *Gaia: A New Look at Life*. Oxford: Oxford University Press.

Macauley, D. (2010). *Elemental Philosophy: Earth, Air, Fire, and Water as Environmental Ideas*. Albany: State University of New York Press.

Manning, J. G. (2018). *The Open Sea: The Economic Life of the Ancient Mediterranean World from the Iron Age to the Rise of Rome*. Princeton, NJ: Princeton University Press.

Marx, P. A. (2011). Athens NM Acropolis 923 and the Contest between Athena and Poseidon for the Land of Attica. *Antike Kunst*, 54, 21–40.

Mauelshagen, F. (2016). Der Verlust der (bio)kulturellen Diversität im Anthropozän. In W. Haber, M. Held and M. Vogt, eds., *Die Welt im Anthropozän. Erkundungen im Spannungsfeld zwischen Ökologie und Humanität*. München: oekom, pp. 39–55.

McInerney, J. & Sluiter, I. (2016). General Introduction. In J. McInerney and I. Sluiter, eds., *Valuing Landscape in Classical Antiquity*. Leiden: Brill, pp. 1–21.

Meyer, M. (2017). *Athena, Göttin von Athen. Kult und Mythos auf der Akropolis bis in klassische Zeit*. Wien: Phoibos Verlag.

Miles, M. M. (2016). Birds around a Temple: Constructing a Sacred Environment. In J. McInerney and I. Sluiter, eds., *Valuing Landscape in Classical Antiquity*. Leiden: Brill, pp. 153–193.

Monks, G., ed. (2017). *Climate Change and Human Responses: A Zooarchaeological Perspective*. Heidelberg: Springer.

Morris, I. (2015). *Foragers, Farmers, and Fossil Fuels: How Human Values Evolve*. Princeton, NJ: Princeton University Press.

Morton, T. (2007). *Ecology without Nature: Rethinking Environmental Aesthetics*. Cambridge, MA: Harvard University Press.

Nash, L. (2006). *Inescapable Ecologies: A History of Environment, Disease, and Knowledge*. Berkeley: University of California Press.

Nash, L. (2017). The Body and Environmental History in the Anthropocene. In U. Heise, J. Christensen and M. Niemann, eds., *The Routledge Companion to the Environmental Humanities*. London: Routledge, 2017, pp. 403–413.

Neils, J. (2012). The Political Process in the Public Festival. In J. R. Brandt and J. W. Iddeng, eds., *Greek and Roman Festivals: Content, Meaning, and Practice*. Oxford: Oxford University Press, pp. 199–215.

Neudecker, R. (2015). Gardens. In R. Raja and J. Rüpke, eds., *A Companion to the Archaeology of Religion in the Ancient World*. Malden, MA: Wiley Blackwell, pp. 220–234.

Nixon, R. (2011). *Slow Violence and the Environmentalism of the Poor*. Cambridge, MA: Harvard UP.

Nixon, R. (2014). The Anthropocene: The Promise and Pitfalls of an Epochal Idea. *edgeeffects Nov. 2014*. edgeeffects.net/anthropocene-promise-and-pitfalls/.

North, D., Wallis, J. & Weingast, B. (2009). *Violence and Social Orders: A Conceptual Framework for Interpreting Recorded Human History*. Cambridge: Cambridge University Press.

Ober, J. (2015). *The Rise and Fall of Classical Greece*. Princeton, NJ: Princeton University Press.

Odling-Smee, F. J. (2003). *Niche Construction: The Neglected Process in Evolution*. Princeton: Princeton University Press.

Oppermann, S. & Iovino, S. (2017). Introduction: The Environmental Humanities and the Challenges of the Anthropocene. In S. Oppermann and S. Iovino, eds., *Environmental Humanities: Voices from the Anthropocene*. Lanham, MD: Rowman & Littlefield, pp. 1–21.

Osborne, R. (2016). Sacrificial Theologies. In E. Eidinow, J. Kindt and R. Osborne, eds., *Theologies of Ancient Greek Religion*. Cambridge: Cambridge University Press, pp. 233–248.

Papachatzis, N. (1989). The Cult of Erechtheus and Athena on the Acropolis of Athens. *Kernos*, 2, 175–185.

Parker, R. (1983). *Miasma: Pollution and Purification in Early Greek Religion*. Oxford: Oxford University Press.

Parker, R. (1987). Myths of Early Athens. In J. Bremmer, ed., *Interpretations of Greek Mythology*. London: Croom Helm, pp. 187–214.

Patay-Horváth, A. (2015). The Contest between Athena and Poseidon. Myth, History and Art. *Historiká. Studi di storia greca e romana*, 5(5), 353–362.

Perrin, B. (1914). *Plutarch: Lives, vol. II*. Cambridge, MA: Harvard University Press.

Petrovic, A. (2015). "Sacred Law". In E. Eidinow and J. Kindt, eds., *The Oxford Handbook of Ancient Greek Religion*. Oxford: Oxford University Press, pp. 339–352.

Plumwood, V. (2002). *Environmental Culture: The Ecological Crisis of Reason*. London: Routledge.

Raaflaub, K. A. (2016). Ancient Greece: Man the Measure of All Things. In K. Raaflaub, ed., *The Adventure of the Human Intellect: Self, Society, and the*

Divine in Ancient World Cultures. Malden, MA: Wiley-Blackwell, pp. 127–148.

Rackham, O. (1996). Ecology and Pseudo-Ecology: The Example of Ancient Greece. In G. Shipley and J. Salmon, eds., *Human Landscapes in Classical Antiquity: Environment and Culture*. London: Routledge, pp. 16–43.

Raja, R. & Rüpke, J. (2015). Archaeology of Religion, Material Religion, and the Ancient World. In R. Raja and J. Rüpke, eds., *A Companion to the Archaeology of Religion in the Ancient World*. Malden, MA: Wiley Blackwell, pp. 1–26.

Rigby, K. (2004). *Topographies of the Sacred. The Poetics of Place in European Romanticism*. Charlottesville, VA: University of Virginia Press.

Rose, D. B., van Dooren, T., Chrulew, M., Cooke, S., Kearnes, M. & O'Gorman, E. (2012). Thinking through the Environment, Unsettling the Humanities. *Environmental Humanities*, 1, 1–5.

Rosenberger, V. (2012). *Religion in der Antike*. Darmstadt: WBG.

Ruddiman, William F. (2003). The Anthropogenic Greenhouse Era Began Thousands of Years Ago. *Climate Change*, 61, 261–293.

Rüpke, J. (2016). *Pantheon: Geschichte der antiken Religionen*. München: Beck.

Sallis, J. (2016). *The Figure of Nature: On Greek Origins*. Bloomington: Indiana University Press.

Salowey, C. A. (2017). Rivers Run through It: Environmental History in Two Heroic Riverine Battles. In G. Hawes, ed., *Myths on the Map: The Storied Landscapes of Ancient Greece*. Oxford: Oxford University Press, pp. 159–177.

Scheer, T., ed. (2019). *Natur – Mythos – Religion im antiken Griechenland*. Stuttgart: Steiner.

Schliephake, Ch. (2017a). Introduction. In Ch. Schliephake, ed., *Ecocriticism, Ecology, and the Cultures of Antiquity*. Lanham, MD: Lexington Books, pp. 1–15.

Schliephake, Ch. (2017b). The Sustainability of Texts: Transcultural Ecology and Classical Reception. In Ch. Schliephake, ed., *Ecocriticism, Ecology, and the Cultures of Antiquity*. Lanham, MD: Lexington Books, pp. 259–278.

Schliephake, Ch. (2019). Ithaca Revisited – Homer's Odyssey and the (Other) Mediterranean Imagination. In M. Brehl, A. Eckl, and K. Platt, eds., *The Mediterranean Other – the other Mediterranean*. Paderborn: Ferdinand Schöningh, pp. 133–151.

Schliephake, Ch., Sojc, N. & Weber, G., eds. (2020). *Nachhaltigkeit in der Antike: Diskurse, Praktiken, Perspektiven*. Stuttgart: Steiner. (forthcoming)

Schneider, S. & Boston, P., eds. (1991). *Scientists on Gaia.* Boston, MA: The MIT Press.

Schwägerl, C. (2014). *The Anthropocene: The Human Era and How It Shapes Our Planet.* Santa Fe, NM: Synergetic Press.

Scott-Phillips, T. C., Laland, K. N., Shuker, D. M., Dickins, T. E. & West, S. A. (2014). The Niche Construction Perspective: A Critical Appraisal. *Evolution,* 68(5), 1231–1243.

Seidler, R. & Bawa, K. S. (2016). Ecology. In J. Adamson, W. A. Gleason and D. Pellow, eds., *Keywords for Environmental Studies.* New York: New York University Press, pp. 71–75.

Siewers, Alfred K., ed. (2014). *Re-Imagining Nature: Environmental Humanities and Ecosemiotics.* Lewisburg: Bucknell University Press.

Simon, E. (1983). *Festivals of Attica: An Archaeological Commentary.* Madison: University of Wisconsin Press.

Smail, D. L. (2008). *On Deep History and the Brain.* New York: Columbia University Press.

Sourvinou-Inwood, C. (2011). *Athenian Myths and Festivals: Aglauros, Erechtheus, Plynteria, Panathenaia, Dionysia,* ed. R. Parker. Oxford: Oxford University Press.

Steffen, W., Grinevald, J., Crutzen, P. J. & McNeill, J. (2011). The Anthropocene: Conceptual and Historical Perspectives. *Philosophical Transactions of the Royal Society A,* 369, 842–867.

Steward, J. H. (1972 [1955]). *Theory of Culture Change: Methodology of Multilinear Evolution.* Urbana: University of Illinois Press.

Stone, C. D. (2010 [1972]). *Should Trees Have Standing? Law, Morality, and the Environment. Third Edition.* Oxford: Oxford University Press.

Thommen, L. 2011. Nachhaltigkeit in der Antike? Begriffsgeschichtliche Überlegungen zum Umweltverhalten der Griechen und Römer. In B. Herrmann, ed., *Beiträge zum Göttinger Umwelthistorischen Kolloquium 2010–2011.* Göttingen: Universitätsverlag Göttingen, pp. 9–24.

Thommen, L. 2012. An Environmental History of Ancient Greece and Rome. Cambridge: Cambridge University Press.

Trépanier, S. (2010). Early Greek Theology: God as Nature and Natural Gods. In J. N. Bremmer and A. Erskine, eds., *The Gods of Ancient Greece: Identities and Transformations.* Edinburgh: Edinburgh University Press, pp. 273–317.

Tress, D. M. (2002). Reuniting Science and Value in the Natural Environment. In T. M. Robinson and L. Westra, eds., *Thinking about the Environment: Our Debt to the Classical and Medieval Past.* Lanham, MD: Lexington Books, pp. 213–221.

Vernant, J.-P. (2016 [1996]). *Mythos und Denken bei den Griechen*. Konstanz: Konstanz University Press.

Vögler, G. (2000). Dachte man in der Antike ökologisch? Mensch und Umwelt im Spiegel antiker Literatur. *Forum Classicum*, 43, 241–253.

von Humboldt, A. (1845–1862). *Kosmos. Entwurf einer physischen Weltbeschreibung, vols. I–V.* Stuttgart: Cotta.

West, M. (1966). *Hesiod. Theogony, ed. with introd. and comm.* Oxford: Clarendon.

Westling, L. (2006). Darwin in Arcadia. Brute Being and the Human Animal Dance from Gilgamesh to Virginia Woolf. *Anglia*, 124(1), 11–43.

Westling, L. & Parham, J. (2017). Introduction. In J. Parham and L. Westling, eds., *A Global History of Literature and the Environment*. Cambridge: Cambridge University Press, pp. 1–17.

White Jr.,L. (1967). The Historical Roots of Our Ecological Crisis. *Science*, 155 (3767), 1203–1207.

Wilson, E. O. (2004 [1978]). *On Human Nature*. Cambridge, MA: Harvard University Press.

Zalasiewicz, J. (2016). The Extraordinary Strata of the Anthropocene. In S. Oppermann and S. Iovino, eds., *Environmental Humanities: Voices from the Anthropocene*. Lanham, MD: Rowman & Littlefield, pp. 115–131.

Zalasiewicz, J., Williams, M., Steffen, W. & Crutzen, P. J. (2010). The New World of the Anthropocene. *Environmental Science & Technology Viewpoint*, 44, 2228–2231.

Zalasiewicz, J., Williams, M. & Waters, C. N. (2016). Anthropocene. In J. Adamson, W. A. Gleason and D. Pellow, eds., *Keywords for Environmental Studies*. New York: New York University Press, pp. 14–16.

Zapf, H. (2016a). Introduction. In H. Zapf, ed., *Handbook of Ecocriticism and Cultural Ecology*. Berlin: De Gruyter, pp. 1–17.

Zapf, H. (2016b). *Literature as Cultural Ecology: Sustainable Texts*. London: Bloomsbury.

Zapf, H. (2017). Cultural Ecology, the Environmental Humanities, and the Transdisciplinary Knowledge of Literature. In S. Oppermann and S. Iovino, eds., *Environmental Humanities: Voices from the Anthropocene*. Lanham, MD: Rowman & Littlefield, pp. 61–80.

Zimmerer, K. S. (1994). Human Geography and the "New Ecology": The Prospect and Promise of Integration. *Annals of the Association of American Geographers*, 84, 108–125.

Acknowledgments

This Element is part of an ongoing discussion that I have been fortunate to lead with teachers, friends, colleagues, and students. I want to thank the editors of the series for giving me the chance of presenting some key points – or, rather, questions – in this framework. I want to thank my colleagues at the University of Augsburg, and especially at the Environmental Science Center (WZU), for lively debate and engaging questions. Over the years, parts of this work have been presented and discussed with colleagues at the Universities of Tübingen, Strasbourg, Kassel, and Berlin. I have benefited greatly from their thoughtful input. All remaining mistakes are my own.

This text is dedicated to the memory of my father-in-law, Henry Waßerberg (1960-2018).

Cambridge Elements ☰

Environmental Humanities

Louise Westling

University of Oregon

Louise Westling is an American scholar of literature and environmental humanities who was a founding member of the Association for the Study of Literature and Environment and its President in 1998. She has been active in the international movement for environmental cultural studies, teaching and writing on landscape imagery in literature, critical animal studies, biosemiotics, phenomenology, and deep history.

Serenella Iovino

University of North Carolina at Chapel Hill

Serenella Iovino is Professor of Italian Studies and Environmental Humanities at the University of North Carolina at Chapel Hill. She has written on a wide range of topics, including environmental ethics and ecocritical theory, bioregionalism and landscape studies, ecofeminism and posthumanism, comparative literature, eco-art, and the Anthropocene.

Timo Maran

University of Tartu

Timo Maran is an Estonian semiotician and poet. Maran is Professor of Ecosemiotics and Environmental Humanities and Head of the Department of Semiotics at the University of Tartu. His research interests are semiotic relations of nature and culture, Estonian nature writing, zoosemiotics and species conservation, and semiotics of biological mimicry.

About the Series

The environmental humanities is a new transdisciplinary complex of approaches to the embeddedness of human life and culture in all the dynamics that characterize the life of the planet. These approaches reexamine our species' history in light of the intensifying awareness of drastic climate change and ongoing mass extinction. To engage this reality, Cambridge Elements in Environmental Humanities builds on the idea of a more hybrid and participatory mode of research and debate, connecting critical and creative fields.

Cambridge Elements ☰

Environmental Humanities

Elements in the Series